How to Grow a Lotus Blossom

or

How a Zen Buddhist Prepares for Death

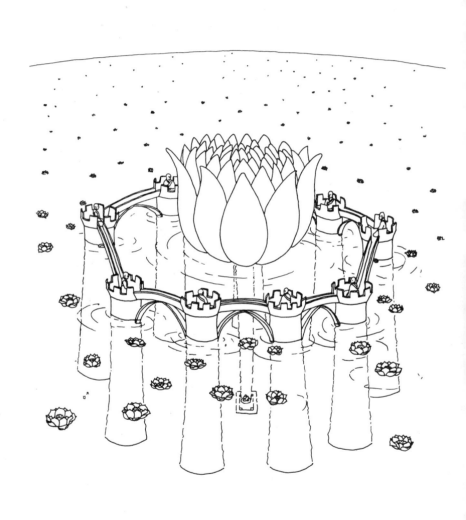

How to Grow a Lotus Blossom
or
How a Zen Buddhist Prepares for Death

by

Rev. P. T. N. H. Jiyu-Kennett, Rōshi

Shasta Abbey
Headquarters of the Reformed Sōtō Zen Church
P.O. Box 478
Mount Shasta, CA 96067

First Edition – May 1977
First Printing – May 1977

Printed in the United States of America.

Some portions of this book have appeared in the
Journal of Shasta Abbey.

Illustrations by Rev. Kōzan Beck,
Rev. Gyokukō Kroenke,
Rev. Hōgetsu Schomberg,
Rev. Kōshin Schomberg,
Rev. Sanshō Runyan.

ISBN 0–930066–01–4

This book is dedicated to the disciple who risked his health to save mine.

ACKNOWLEDGMENTS.

The author wishes to thank the following people who have contributed much of their time and effort towards the preparation and publication of this book:

Manuscript preparation, editing, and consultation:—
Revs. Jitsudō Baran, Kyogen Carlson, Mokurai Cherlin, Ekō Little, Daizui MacPhillamy, Mokudai Millar, Sanshō Runyan, Isan Sacco, Kōshin and Hōgetsu Schomberg, and Haryo Young; Saul and Majid Barodofsky; and Dr. Robert Frager.
Typing, Typesetting, and Layout:—
Revs. Gyojin Essex and Kōmei Larson.
Art and Graphics:—
Revs. Kōzan Beck, Gyokukō Kroenke, Hōgetsu and Kōshin Schomberg, and Sanshō Runyan, who drew the pictures as exactly as they could, as I described them.
I am also grateful to the authors and publishers of the various works I have referred to, as acknowledged in the text.

CONTENTS.

	Page
Frontispiece:— The Mandala of the Lotus,	
Foreword,	vii.
Kenshōs,	1.
How to Use this Book,	9.
Zazen Rules,	10.
Plate I:— The End of the Road,	15.
Plate II:— Scaling the Glass Mountains,	19.
Plate III:— The Only Way Left,	21.
Plate IV:— The Road Appears,	23.
Plate V:— Entry to the Abyss,	25.
Plate VI:— Heaven is the Most Dangerous of All Places,	29.
Plate VII:— The Voice of the Eternal Lord,	33.
Plate VIII:— The Lake of Quietism,	37.
Plate IX:— Vast Emptiness,	51.
Plate X:— The Army of Mara,	57.
Plate XI:— The Appearance of the Mandala,	61.
Plate XII:— The Growing Mandala,	63.
Plate XIII:— The Source of the Kōan,	66.
Plate XIV:— Appearance in the Hall of Shadows,	71.
Plate XV & XVI:— The Spirit Rises to Greet the Lord,	74.
Plates XVII, XVIII, XIX:— Struck by the Sword of Buddha's Wisdom,	77.
Plate XX:— The Time of Segaki,	83.
Plates XXI & XXII:— Recognition in the Waveless Sea,	88.
Plate XXIII:— The Lord's Will,	93.
Plate XXIV:— Do Not Stay in Heaven,	98.

Page

Plates XXV & XXVI:— Ordination and
    Graduation,   104.
Plate XXVII:— The Five Aspects of the Monk,   111.
Plates XXVIII, XXIX, XXX:— Receiving the
    Teaching,   117.
Plate XXXI:— The Iron Man,   123.
Plate XXXII:— The True Being,   128.
Plate XXXIII:— The Real Monk,   133.
Plate XXXIV:— The First Column—Eternal
    Meditation,   135.
Plate XXXV:— The Second Column—The
    Cleansing Water of the Spirit,   139.
Plate XXXVI:— The Third Column—Heaven
    Penetrates Earth,   143.
Plate XXXVII:— The Fourth Column—Bathed
    in the Fountain of the Lord,   151.
Plate XXXVIII:— The Fifth Column—The
    Buddha Within,   156.
Plate XXXIX:— The Path of the Lotus,   161.
Plate XL:— Heaven and Earth Are One,   167.
Plate XLI:— Nothing Matters,   173.
Plate XLII:— The Lord of the House,   179.
Plate XLIII:— Not Emptiness, Not Fullness,
    Not Circular, Not Spatial,   181.
Postword,   184.
Appendix A:— The Flow of the Breath During
    Meditation,   186.
Appendix B:— "The Life of the Hasidim,"   196.
Appendix C:— The *Hui Ming Ching*,   228.
Appendix D:— Questions and Answers,   251.
Glossary Compiled by Rev. Mokurai Cherlin,   268.

FOREWORD.

This book is the result of a year-long retreat of intensive meditation by Rev. Jiyu-Kennett, Rōshi, Abbess of Shasta Abbey and spiritual head of the Reformed Sōtō Zen Church. Thirteen years previously Rev. Kennett experienced, at Sōji-ji Temple in Japan, the first great kenshō, or enlightenment experience, which caused her master, the Very Reverend Keidō Chisan Kōhō, Zenji, to certify her as his Dharma Heir and, several years later, qualify her as a Rōshi and fully-licensed Teacher of Sōtō Zen Buddhism. During the succeeding thirteen years her master died and she moved to the United States where she founded Shasta Abbey near Mt. Shasta, California, and served as its Abbess, ordaining and training priests of the Reformed Sōtō Zen Church.

During the autumn of 1975, Kennett Rōshi began to fall ill, suffering from increasing water retention, diabetes, high blood pressure and cardiac irregularity. By April of 1976 she had become too ill to continue with her duties as Abbess of Shasta Abbey but she went to Los Angeles to rest and to conduct several university lectures. Consulting a specialist in internal medicine she was informed that she could expect to die of a heart attack within as little as three months if her condition continued unimproved. This was the first of three events which led her to embark upon this year of intensive meditation. A week later the illness became markedly worse and she was forced to confine herself to bed. At this point the disciple whom she had regarded as her chief descendent, and upon whom she was relying for aid, felt unable to continue and departed. This second shock caused her condition to worsen further and she came to our nearest temple, in Oakland, California, so as to be able to die within a temple of our Church. I happened to be the acting Prior of that temple at the time and we were at least able to offer her a room to herself and a certain amount of peace and quiet. During her first week in Oakland Kennett Rōshi contacted a friend who was a doctor and he suggested that she see a practitioner of an esoteric Oriental healing art. Unfortunately this man immediately pronounced to Kennett Rōshi that her teaching and way of life were wrong, were the cause of her illness and that the only cure was to cease everything and put herself entirely in his hands. Faced first with the prospect of imminent death, second with no heir to carry on the teaching and third with the possibility that everything had been wrong, she decided to meditate as deeply and continuously as possible, to examine every moment of her life and to find out absolutely, no matter what the cost to her health and life, if all she had learned from her master, all she had done and all she had passed on to her disciples was false.

From this moment Kennett Rōshi meditated with all her remaining strength. For four months she almost never left her little room in Oakland. She formally resigned all duties as Abbess of Shasta Abbey and we permitted no one to see her or have contact with her except two or three of her eldest disciples and a very kind friend who came twice a week to give her a relaxing form of Oriental massage. At her request not even her doctor was allowed to interrupt her meditation retreat and she took none of his medications, relying solely upon her meditation and a few simple foods and herbs. The first twelve plates of this book tell the story of what happened to Kennett Rōshi in her meditation during those months. The remaining thirty-one plates describe her experiences during her meditation after her return to Shasta Abbey.

During this year it was my privilege to be with Kennett Rōshi much of the time, nursing her during the first four months and as her assistant after her return to Shasta Abbey. The experiences which she describes in the plates of this book represent critical moments in the meditation—the moments of receiving the teaching which the Buddhas and Patriarchs provided through the experience of her senses. In her case these came as complete visual and sensory experiences; however, I know well that Kennett Rōshi did not undertake this meditation in order to have such experiences, nor did she spend most of her time involved with them, nor are they even necessary. What is important, and what I saw Kennett Rōshi doing most of this year, are the things which made it possible for her to receive, understand and follow such teaching. First was her complete and continual willingness to give up everything—to risk everything including her life—in order to know the Truth absolutely. Second was the looking at every detail of her life all the way back to birth to find, face and *do something*, if possible, about each instance in which she had broken any of the Buddha's Precepts. To this Kennett Rōshi devoted great energy during the first few months and she has done this any time subsequently that she has remembered another instance of a mistake, no matter how small, in the keeping of the Precepts. Then came the complete re-commitment to practice Preceptual Truth continuously every day henceforth for the rest of her life. (She made this commitment first when she had her kenshō in Japan.) It was not enough to clean up everything once in preparation for death; every act *must* be in harmony with the Three Pure Precepts: do no harm; do only that which is good; do good for others. Fourth came the willingness to look back past birth to see the karma of previous lives in order to learn from the mistakes those previous beings made and to find compassion for them so as not to repeat their errors and so as to cut forever the roots of karma. Then came absolute receptiveness to the will of the Buddhas—the immediate and heart-felt "YES" to any request or teaching of the Lord of the House—the willingness to follow absolutely and without even the thought of doubt the "still small voice" of the Truth no matter where it might lead. Sixth came her resolution to share these things with others, regardless of whether they put them to good use or whether they rejected them utterly. Even the grief caused by the turning away of a few disciples did not stop her from sharing the Truth, always with care not to hurt others. The Precept which says, "Do not be mean in sharing the wealth of the Dharma," must be kept as absolutely as the other Precepts, as must the Bodhisattva Vow of helping all beings regardless of the cost to oneself. I know that this book was written from this motive in the hope that it may benefit not only those who are ill and dying, and those who work with them, but also such students of Buddhism as desire to make the absolute commitment necessary to deepen their religious training in this way.

The book begins with the translation of Dōgen Zenji's "Zazen Rules" taken from Kennett Rōshi's book *Zen is Eternal Life*. This, together with the Appendix on meditation, should be studied in detail as it is the *foundation* of the practice of meditation from which all the rest of the book came forth. Those who wish to use this as a means of deepening their meditation should start by becoming thoroughly familiar with the "Zazen Rules" and put them into daily practice. They should also make daily practical use of the instructions for following the breath given in the Appendix. Above all, do not try to have the same experiences that are described in the plates of this book. The experiences will differ for each person and, for some, there may not be such experiences at all. What is important is the *willingness* to enter deeply into meditation and religious training and to learn from *whatever* means of teaching the Buddhas and Patriarchs may provide. The experiences described here are of great use to read in order to see the sequence in which the teaching comes and to see how one person learned from the teaching of the senses. If you misunderstand their use and meditate in order to have similar experiences I assure you that you will succeed only in deluding yourself.

The message to those who may be seriously ill, or dying, (and to those who work with them) is quite clear. First, do not fear to face the possibility of imminent death; if you wish to know the Truth and die in peace everything must be faced squarely, including the fact of death itself. Second, do not despair; when you really know that you are facing death you have nothing to lose by reviewing your life and your karma completely, setting right what you can and devoting yourself to deep meditation. This can be the best possible moment to know the Lord! The accounts of people who have been revived after clinical death (see, for example, *Life After Life* by Raymond A. Moody, Jr., Mockingbird Books, Atlanta, Georgia, 1975) state that this process of review happens anyway at the time of death. Why wait; *now* you still have time to act to set things right and to come to a far deeper and more beautiful understanding of the Truth of life. Third, do not fear to follow the teachings of your Heart. The Buddhist scriptures say that we enter death alone accompanied only by our good and evil karma. If you hold on to, or worry about, the opinions of others, or whether what you do may shorten your life, how can you be free to follow the teaching of the Lord of the House completely and so be at one with Him and at peace? Finally, understand that, although these meditations are not done in an attempt to cure illness, there appear to be some conditions which are improved by them. Thus it can sometimes occur that a person who meditates deeply, and cleans up his life completely, will not only find deeper peace but may also discover a new purpose to life and the time and strength with which to fulfill it.

The forty-three plates in this book are not the end of the journey, just as they are not the only way in which this teaching may come about. One thing that has been clear all during these meditations is that they are but "the tip of the iceberg." As anyone who has ever had a kenshō knows well, it is not the end of religious training—it is a new beginning. This is true of the kenshō-in-slow-motion which is described in this book. It is also true that there are millions of beings in the sea of lotus blossoms of Plates XXI and XXII, and more are being born into it daily; Kennett Rōshi is neither the first nor the only person to understand this teaching, nor is it limited to students of Zen, nor even to Buddhists. This leads naturally to the question of whether or not this teaching is true Zen, especially since it is being taught by a woman. With regard to the latter point I would quote Dōgen Zenji, thirteenth-century founder of the Sōtō Zen Sect in Japan, "A little girl of seven even may be the teacher of the four classes of Buddhists and the mother of True Compassion to all living things" ("Shushōgi," section four). Is it Zen? Historically, some Zen masters have reported experiences such as this, others have not. Do not be worried by forms and appearances; the essence of this teaching is clearly Zen, as can be deduced from reading the works of the Zen Patriarchs and as can be known directly by any serious student of Zen who has experienced, at least once, his innate enlightenment. Ultimately you must be the judge of whether this book is good for you. If you wish, practice the form of Zen meditation suggested herein wholeheartedly and then see if the results are good; that is really the only way that you can know.

After this year of meditation it is my pleasure to say that Kennett Rōshi's health has improved and indeed become vigorous. She has lost about fifty pounds of retained water; her diabetes has disappeared; her blood pressure is below the norm for her age; and her EKG has returned to normal. She has the prospect of a long and active life and she is again serving as Abbess of Shasta Abbey and the spiritual director of our Church. It was not for this, however, that she undertook these meditations and it is not merely for a long and active life that I recommend them to you. If you wish to grow the lotus blossom of Buddha's Wisdom, and if you wish to know the Eternal Lord and meet Him with a pure heart, both now and at the hour of death, I pray that you may meditate deeply and that you may find this book of use.

Daizui MacPhillamy
Shasta Abbey
Mt. Shasta, California
December 22, 1976

KENSHŌS.

Enlightenment is not experienced in stages, nor
are there types of enlightenment, it is an on-going flow,
therefore the word 'type' in the chapter is a misnomer
and is only used for convenience because there is no
adequate word.

On October 5th., 1962, I experienced the kenshō[1]
which caused Zenji Keidō Chisan Kōhō[2] to qualify me
as a teacher of Zen. Although I did not receive the actual qualification until several years later, after I had
learned how to do the actual teaching, it was this kenshō which made that qualification possible. The type
of kenshō experience I had at this time is the most
usual and, to my knowledge, is the one upon which
most of the present teachers of Zen in the orient and,
possibly, those in America too, have their qualifica-
tions based. It should, however, be understood clearly
that there are other types of kenshō besides this one.
Unfortunately documentation of such experiences,
other than the first type, is extraordinarily scant; hence
the tremendous amount of misconception and mystique
surrounding them. It occurred to me, therefore, that a
book in English was much to be desired on this subject,
showing clearly the various stages that such later experiences take.

The kenshō I experienced in 1962 is the "great
flash of deep understanding,"—the Kanzeon or "Pene-

---

1. This is translatable as enlightenment experience,
realisation or understanding.
2. Kennett Rōshi's master.

tration of Heaven" kenshō as it is called. It is the one in which one *knows* one's unity with the immaculacy of nothingness and which grows ever deeper if one keeps up one's meditation *and* training. It is the result of much serious training, either in a monastery or in the world itself, and is exemplified in the eighth Ox-Herding Picture,[3] the previous seven making clear the sort of training necessary to reach this state. I have described how it happened to me at some length in "The Wild, White Goose."[4]

What happens as a result of constant training after the first kenshō may be called the On-Going Fūgen kenshō. This one, because of its almost imperceptible growth, is not associated in the mind with any *one* event although certain "little moments that make one dance" are signs of it. In many ways the time between the first and third kenshōs is the most difficult, as anyone who has had a first kenshō knows, for the simple reason that the temptations to break the Precepts are much greater and far more subtle. The norm of human behaviour being set at what psychologists consider "healthy," i.e. a person is well integrated and adjusted if he has a reasonable ego and a fair swatch each of greed, hate and delusion with a little lukewarm morality thrown in, is of little comfort to one who has had a first kenshō and finds that, in order to progress further, he must now not only *keep* his passions rooted out but also clean up the impregnations that they have left upon his skhandas both in this life and in his previous ones. A whole book could be written about the problems that beset a person during this period and I may write one at a later date.

---

3. The Empty Circle.
4. Kennett Rōshi's diary of her years in Japan.

The third type of kenshō about which, as I have said, almost nothing to my knowledge is written needs much more explanation and documentation. Let me state, at the outset, that what I have set down here as my personal experience is, in no way, exclusive to me. Absolutely anyone who trains seriously, who makes the Precepts[5] his blood and bones and who not only tries to *live* by them but cleans up all the impregnations, both of his present life and of his past lives, that the breakage of those Precepts has left upon his skhandas, can experience this type of kenshō.

There is, however, one important point that should be mentioned here. In the first kenshō one goes through all the stages mentioned in this book as taking place in the third kenshō with this difference:— in the first kenshō the stages flash by so quickly that the whole kenshō is only comprehended as one flash. One goes, as it were, from earth to heaven by rocket, or a lightning bolt, with no time to take notice of the journey before one has arrived. The third kenshō takes place slowly and deliberately with plenty of time to comprehend each step of the way. For example in the first kenshō one jumps of necessity beyond the opposites and *knows* for ever afterwards that one *has* jumped. In the third kenshō the opposites are each looked at slowly and dispassionately and then *deliberately* discarded; the first kenshō is a swift comprehension of grace; the third kenshō *starts* as a *deliberate* act of will.

It has been taught in the West that all experiences, visual or otherwise, during meditation should be regarded as makyo and taken no notice of whatsoever. Whereas this is true for *all* who have *not* had a first kenshō, it is not *necessarily* true for those who have

5. Please see Plate VIII for a complete explanation of the Buddhist Precepts.

the little flashes of what I here call the On-Going Fûgen kenshô and not true at all for those having the third kenshô. The Zen masters of old did not talk about the valid experiences, however, for fear that new trainees would mistake makyo for the real thing. There are places in the Scriptures where they are mentioned but, for some reason, people nowadays get upset when a Zenist mentions them and I do not doubt that many will be annoyed with me for doing so. At *any* stage of training it is very dangerous to *cling* to experiences, whether they be makyo or valid. The valid ones should be understood clearly and then left behind; the *purpose* of meditation is the harmonisation of body and mind—that experiences do, or do not, occur whilst this is happening is neither here nor there. Dōgen Zenji, to my knowledge, never had *visual* experiences; Keizan Zenji had many; they *both* stressed the importance of meditation and *both* reached the same spiritual place. Always one *feels* what happens during the third kenshô. Incidentally, the master knows in his own body and mind if a trainee's kenshô is real if he is present at the *time* the kenshô takes place; if he is not then he has to observe and study the disciple with care, and test him in many subtle ways in order to be sure of his realisation as pointed out in *Zen is Eternal Life*. Zen masters are not sorcerers.

When I was quite young I can remember talking about kenshôs with D. T. Suzuki in London and wondering exactly why, since enlightenment is one and undivided, it was necessary to have more than one kenshô. I remember asking him if, since a Zen master never says he is *enlightened*, he *knew* that he had had a kenshô and he assured me that he did. I also remember asking him, "Have *you* ever had this experience yourself?" and he admitted that he had. Later that same year he said openly and clearly, "Once or twice I have had the

4

great experience but a million times the little moments that make one dance." Between the great kenshōs come the millions of "little moments that make one dance" that make up the On-Going Fūgen kenshō,— the moments that remind you, any time you get really down, that you *have* experienced the Penetration of Heaven kenshō. I myself have experienced them many times; I know them well. I also know that D. T. Suzuki did not mind openly admitting that he had had *kenshō* experience nor did any of the great Zen masters I met in the east. It is perfectly true that they did *not*, however, say that they were enlightened. They only admitted to having experienced kenshō. There is a great deal of difference in saying that you have experienced kenshō and in saying that you are enlightened; I would like to make this point very clear. Kenshō experience, even the second type through its tiny moments, can be fixed in time; enlightenment is an on-going process, ever-flowing like a river. You cannot hold a river within your hand but you can trail your hand in the river. By grasping you lose all; by letting the flow continue you possess all whilst possessing nothing. My own master did make an announcement concerning my kenshō the day after my Transmission Ceremony. This is quite customary in Zen monasteries especially if the master intends to train the person as a future teacher of Zen. I make these comments because I know there is a prevalent belief, or there was, certainly, some years ago when I was in England, that this subject must never, or should never, be talked about. I do not know from whence this idea came; I certainly did not find it anywhere in the east.

I suspect that people go through the type of experience I describe later in this book during their final illness and shortly before their death. The Zen master, however, having learned to meditate properly and overcome his fear of death or, perhaps I should say, being more anxious for the harmonisation of his body and mind than worrying about what will happen should he meditate too deeply, can have this experience without necessarily having to die, as indeed can any other being who is willing to go very deeply into meditation *and* training; this kenshō can only take place as a result of *both being equal in intensity.*

It is not good to do deep meditation and training completely by oneself as the reader will discover as he reads on; nor is it wise to be in any place whatsoever where he can be much disturbed. The world is always anxious to push its way in when someone wishes to do something about himself. When advanced spiritual development is reached the world seems to treble and quadruple its efforts to distract and dishearten, as the reader will very soon find out, and it is then that faith in the memory of the first kenshō is absolutely vital; one second of doubt, even the possibility of *thinking of the possibility of doubting*, can cause the spirit to despair and death is the result. True meditation is not for cowards; it is hazardous, perilous and magnificent. For this reason a place of absolute peace and quiet is necessary. You will also need a friend or a disciple who is perfectly willing to go to any lengths to keep the world from bothering you.

There is absolutely no doubt in my mind that other religious traditions have a similar type of experience to these three kenshōs which their adherents understand within their own framework of beliefs. There is a book in existence, *The Secret of the Golden Flower*,[6] a translation of a Taoist text, which speaks very clearly

---

6. Translated by Richard Wilhelm, with Commentary by C. G. Jung, Harcourt, Brace & World, Inc., New York, 1962.

of a meditative experience almost identical to mine but in totally different terminology. Unfortunately the book only seems to speak of four stages as opposed to forty-three that I mention here; but they are four very important ones. Also included in the book is a somewhat muddled attempt at explanation by Dr. Jung that the reader would do well to skip. The manuscript itself is couched in alchemical terminology and the person meditating seems, to my mind, to be doing it for doubtful reasons, i.e. longevity, but the manuscript is very useful for comparison. If Taoism knew of this, and this particular manuscript says quite clearly that the Buddhists speak of it in the Avatamsaka and Surangama, it would seem to me to be perfectly normal that Christianity, Islam, Judaism and other religions should know of it also.

It is very essential, if a person has a similar experience to mine, that he does *not* suffer from the idea that he is the one and only to ever experience it. *Nor must he cling to the experience.* The thing that gave me the greatest joy during this time was the realisation that I was *not* the one and only lotus blossom in the lake,—that there were *millions* of others there before me and *millions* more coming up.

This brings me to another matter. I do not doubt that every person *sees* and *experiences* this somewhat *differently* to me, although the *stages* for doing so are *identically* the same. It is the *stages* of this particular path that the reader should carefully study, not so that he can have *my* experience but so that he may have his *own*. In a way these experiences are a much more elaborate and deeper version of the original Ox-Herding Pictures. The reader should also know that he must not undertake meditation for the purpose of *having* this type of experience. I had no idea that I would experience this. All I knew was that, if I were going to die, I was going to do the finest job of it I possibly could; that I did not die happens to be a bonus; that I experienced this is an absolute joy for which my gratitude has no bounds. It is my sincere hope that this type of kenshō will become much more widely known and, as a result of very serious and hard training, much more often experienced. One must, however, go on beyond the experiences; they should be *learned* from but *not* clung to. The teaching is all that matters.

One last word—fear of being laughed at, fear of being regarded as a publicity-seeker or a crank, fear of what the world may think may stop a lot of people from writing down, and being willing to admit to and share, what they do experience. I personally feel this to be wrong. In a day and age when far too many people are terrified of death, perhaps far too few are willing to admit to what they, themselves, have experienced when brought back from the door of death and far too many are afraid of what the medical professions and others will say if they speak of their experiences. If those who have experienced these things speak out much fear can be removed, much joy can be experienced and much grief prevented. For these reasons I wish to share with the reader this great experience.

HOW TO USE THIS BOOK.

The blueprint for doing Zazen [Fukanzazengi] that follows should be studied with great care in connection with the plates and descriptions herein. Plates I-XIII could also be compared to parts 1-3 of Appendix C, always remembering that Appendix C is Taoist and not Buddhist; Plate XIV to part 4; Plates XV-XXVI to part 5; Plates XXVII-XXXI to part 6; Plates XXXIX-XLII to part 7 and Plate XLIII to part 8. The teaching engendered by the *non-clinging* to the first seven plates is given in the explanation of Plate VIII; the teaching given by the *non-clinging* to Plates IX-XXXIV is given in Plate XXXV.

"The Life of the Hasidim" (Appendix B) may also be compared with these forty-three plates.

The Zazen Rules, or Fukanzazengi, are the explanation of the physical and mental attitude required for true meditation.

ZAZEN RULES (FUKANZAZENGI).[1]

Why are training and enlightenment differentiated since the Truth is universal? Why study the means to attaining it since the supreme teaching is free? Since Truth is seen to be clearly apart from that which is unclean, why cling to a means of cleansing it? Since Truth is not separate from training, training is unnecessary—however, the separation will be as that between heaven and earth if even the slightest gap exists—WHEN THE OPPOSITES ARISE THE BUDDHA MIND IS LOST. However much you may be proud of your understanding, however much you may be enlightened, whatever your attainment of wisdom and supernatural power, your finding of the way to mind illumination, your power to touch heaven and to enter into enlightenment, when the opposites arise you have almost lost the way to salvation. Although the Buddha had great wisdom at birth, He sat in training for six years; although Bodhidharma Transmitted the Buddha Mind, we still hear the echoes of his nine years facing a wall. The Ancestors were very diligent and there is no reason why we people of the present day cannot understand. All you have to do is cease from erudition, withdraw within and reflect upon yourself. Should you be able to cast off body and mind naturally the Buddha Mind will immediately manifest itself; if you want to find it quickly you must start at once.

You should meditate in a quiet room, eat and drink moderately, cut all ties, give up everything, think

---

1. This is a Zen scripture written by Dōgen Zenji which is recited each evening in Zen temples.

of neither good nor evil, consider neither right nor wrong. Control mind function, will, consciousness, memory, perception and understanding; you must not strive thus to become Buddha. Cling to neither sitting nor lying down. Place a round cushion on top of a thick square one on your seat. Some people meditate in the full-lotus position and others in the half-lotus one. In the full-lotus position your right foot is placed upon your left thigh and your left foot is placed upon your right thigh; in the half-lotus position the left foot is placed upon the right thigh and nothing more; do not wear tight clothing. Rest the right hand on the left foot and the left hand in the palm of the right hand with the thumbs touching lightly; sit upright, leaning neither to left nor right, backwards nor forwards. The ears must be in line with the shoulders and the nose in line with the navel; the tongue must be held lightly against the back of the top teeth with the lips and teeth closed. Keep the eyes open, breathe in quickly, settle the body comfortably and breathe out sharply. Sway the body left and right then sit steadily with the legs crossed, neither trying to think nor trying not to think. Just sitting, with no deliberate thought, is the important aspect of Zazen.

This type of Zazen is not something that is done in stages of meditation; it is simply the lawful gateway to carefree peace. To train and enlighten ourselves is to become thoroughly wise; the kōan appears *naturally* in daily life. If you become thus utterly free you will be as the water wherein the dragon dwells or as the mountain whereon the tiger roams. Understand clearly that the Truth appears naturally and then your mind will be free from doubts and vacillation. When you wish to arise from Zazen sway the body gently from side to side and arise quietly; the body must make no violent movement; I myself have seen that the ability to die whilst sitting and standing, which transcends both peasant and sage, is obtained through the power of Zazen. It is no more possible to understand natural activity with the discriminatory mind than it is possible to understand the signs of enlightenment; nor is it possible to understand training and enlightenment by supernatural means; such understanding is outside the realm of speech and vision, such Truth is beyond discrimination. Do not discuss the wise and the ignorant, there is only one thing—to train hard for this is true enlightenment; training and enlightenment are naturally undefiled; to live by Zen is the same as to live an ordinary daily life. The Buddha Seal has been preserved by both the Buddhas in the present world and by those in the world of the Indian and Chinese Patriarchs, they are thus always spreading true Zen—all activity is permeated with pure Zazen—the means of training are thousandfold but pure Zazen must be done. It is futile to travel to other dusty countries thus forsaking your own seat; if your first step is false you will immediately stumble. Already you are in possession of the vital attributes of a human being—do not waste time with this and that—*you* can possess the authority of Buddha. Of what use is it to merely enjoy this fleeting world? This body is as transient as dew on the grass, life passes as swiftly as a flash of lightning, quickly the body passes away, in a moment life is gone. O sincere trainees, do not doubt the true dragon, do not spend so much time in rubbing only a part of the elephant; look *inwards* and advance directly along the road that leads to the Mind, respect those who have reached the goal of goalessness, become one with the wisdom of the Buddhas, *Transmit* the wisdom of the Patriarchs. If you do these things for some time you will become as herein described, then the Treasure House will open naturally and you will enjoy it fully.

PLATE I:– THE END OF THE ROAD.

(The plates are a close representation of what I experienced. It should be understood that the first six represent the first twelve days of meditation and are an attempt to capture, in tableau, what was actually a moving scene. For example, I spent two days and nights meditating on the two roads and listening to the reasons for and against climbing the mountains, and another two days and nights in the actual climb. The decisions needed for each stage were always taken at sundown which is when each stage (i.e. plate) should be considered as starting. Plates, or stages, seven to nine cover a period of two months, plates ten to twelve a further period of a month and a half and plates thirteen to forty-three I experienced after I had regained my health over a period of several weeks.)

I have been fading steadily for some time. A masseuse came and eased some of the tensions in me a little and some herbal teas have helped somewhat with the water elimination but my disciple, Daizui, has watched me drift further and further away and now finally cries out in his own anguish for help for all of us. Miracle of miracles! His cry is heard by the Lord of the House and he experiences the first great kenshō— that which is known as the Kanzeon or Penetration of Heaven. Instead of my former heir who had deserted me and who, although he was close to understanding, had not yet experienced kenshō, I now have a true heir whom I can certify. This had to be done at once lest I die before he received the seals. I Transmitted him here on my sickbed and called witnesses for the sealing.

How awe-ful is this Penetration of Heaven; how foolish are men to think that they can solve the kōan with their own puny minds. Not until they give up their egos of themselves and put their trust solely in the Lord of the House does the kōan solve itself. Now I may indeed go into meditation. I have cut my other disciples loose so that no one may harm them; I could become so ill that others may issue orders in my name without my knowledge and consent. I have resigned from the temple and now again am an unsui—and I have Daizui, my true heir, who is nursing me. I have not even the strength left to talk to him.

As I go deep into meditation two roads appear and a great mountain range. On the road to the left, there are more women than men for their inadequacy is great and they believe they can get nowhere whatsoever unless a man helps them. Their world is the world of soap-opera, of television, of gossip, of being enmeshed absolutely in their family life. There are *some* men upon this road too but women outnumber them three to one. To the right is the road that leads to expensive entertainment, to high worldly success, to learning, to universities, to great places in the world of men, great names in politics and art and, on this road, men outnumber women three to one for they believe, in their complacency, that they are adequate, that all the best things are their prerogative; yet they are trapped as much as are the women. The women believe they cannot move without a man because they are inadequate and the men do not move because they believe they do not need to. Adequacy and inadequacy are equally dangerous traps. For both men and women it becomes steadily more obvious that something is missing, something is needed. After all where do these roads lead? Entertainments are an unreality as are worldly success, money, fame and fortune; all these things are but temporary placebos; when death comes it has to be faced alone. The great entertainments, the great names, the great learning can do nothing then, any more than can the man in which a woman placed her trust; he cannot save her at the hour of death. Behind me is what passes for religion; it tries to tell me how and why but has no answers to my real questions.

And yet these roads beckon me and something in me says, "Choose one. You still have *some* time left. Enjoy it; there is nothing you can do." And another voice says, "Take no notice of those roads. Know that nothing *really* matters. Be mindful." I am in terror but I heed the latter voice. Something vaguely remembered from the kenshō in 1962 bids me go on. Am I imagining this? Do *not* doubt that kenshō; it *did* happen; *go on!*

So, refusing to go down either road, I see nothing but the great mountain range before me. Over these mountains heavy storms rage. The mountain faces are sheer like glass. How can they be scaled by a being that has no knowledge of how to climb, no rope, no means of grasping the glassy surface?

PLATE II:– SCALING THE GLASS MOUNTAINS.

There is nothing for it but to go straight up the face. How do I climb that which is sheer and glassy? By going straight up, by not thinking whether I will live or die, by not thinking I am inadequate or adequate, male or female. Maleness and femaleness cannot help me here; here the world of the opposites ceases. There is no way up for one who is stuck in inadequacy or in adequacy.

Up and up and up, without ever doubting my ability, without looking down, without thinking, without caring about the lightning that comes from the storms, without fearing the ferocious animals that I may meet, without worrying about the darkness or the avalanches, holding fast to the memory of the kenshō; up, up and on. Will the climb to the top never end? Perhaps everyone else was right, perhaps to go off into despair—but I *know* this is wrong and will not listen to the little voice that says, "Go back. You are too weak, you cannot do it. You have not been good enough to climb this mountain; you have not done enough to train yourself—you do not know how to climb." And I say, "Quiet. I *can* climb and I *will*."

PLATE III:– THE ONLY WAY LEFT.

The mountains seem endless now that the face has been scaled. From their summit one can see the roads on either side—cheap entertainments and family life on one side, expensive entertainments, fame and fortune on the other, each leading off to the same place—despair. I can see it clearly from up here. And yet what have *I* got? Nothing but rocks and boulders. On hands and knees, injured by the rocks, I go on; cut by volcanic glass, hands and feet and knees bleeding and torn, on and on—and, on each side, the bright lights beckoning; but they go off into darkness and despair. Better by far to bleed upon the mountains; better by far to trust in, and remember, the kenshō.

PLATE IV:— THE ROAD APPEARS.

The mountain top seems to be flattening out and descending to the level of the roads. They can still be seen on either side through gaps in the rock; perilous gaps, narrow and spiny, small holes. But anyone who is on the roads can make it through if he or she so wishes; there is always a way onto this mountain range. The stones become smaller and smaller. I am still on hands and knees, the bleeding and the cutting continue. I must take no notice of what is on either side. I must remember that one can go out through those holes just as much as one can come in and take no notice, take no notice whatsoever. Absolute blackness beyond me and straight ahead. The bright lights on either side become dimmer and dimmer; I must take no notice of them; not see their beckoning; go on, go on, go on.

PLATE V:– ENTRY TO THE ABYSS.

The blackness is complete. It is as if I am in a huge tunnel; everywhere darkness and blackness. Still on hands and knees I move on until, in front of me, there looms a great, black lotus; it towers high above me, huge, incredible. Within me a voice whispers, "Be careful,–be *very* careful. Remember, *nothing* matters." Upon the side of the lotus is written in dull, yet glowing, red, "*NOTHING MATTERS*." Ahead and to the left I perceive dimly a giant, iron pillar that I know penetrates the universe.

A taunting voice inside me says, "Better by far to jump into that great, black lotus, to enter the abyss of despair. What point is there in going on, bleeding and cut and torn? Jump in, why not?" The first voice says, "You have no reason to do that." The other says, "Why not?" "There is a beautiful tree outside; it is a beautiful evening," says Daizui when I ask him why I should continue to live. "What have I to do with these things?" I reply. "What is the point?" A voice comes from the pillar, "It is not my problem that you fall into despair; it does not matter to me that you die. I am eternal. It does not matter in the least if you should die. Go ahead if you wish; jump into the abyss." "But I do not want to die!" I cry, "I do not want to die!" I draw back from the abyss, from the great, black lotus towering in front of me. Remember, nothing matters.... Remember, nothing matters.... Remember the scriptures– Mindfulness is all–over the mountains, up to this black abyss, that which matters most–mindfulness is all– AND–nothing matters. The scriptures must be taken literally for they were obviously obtained at death's door. In red letters flashes across my mind, "Never come too close nor put yourself too far away; do not come too close to the abyss and do not put yourself too far away from it." It is important to always remember that the abyss exists otherwise one will become safe in one's own mind and not notice falling into it.

As I stand before it, for now I am standing up, I know that if life comes there is only life and if death comes there is only death. I step off into death when my purpose for living ceases; I will not step off into death for I do not wish to die. "The secret of life is will; words are its key." This is the darkest moment that a being can know. If I had not seen the cleanness of the water thirteen years ago[1] I would not now be able to have the faith to walk this road. The only way I can go on is if I put right every wrong act that I have ever committed. I tear into my past and drag it naked and trembling into the light. I cleanse my karma of body, mouth and will with the tears of repentance and actual reparation for that which has not been taken care of since my first kenshō. This is the deeper meaning of the first of the Buddha's Noble Truths, Suffering Exists. No act of omission or commission, covert or overt, must be left out if I would go on—and I *will* go on—no matter what the cost, the pain or the shame.

Days have passed and the searching of my heart continues, as it must always continue, even should I survive this, for this cleansing is not something that ceases—always there will be things I have forgotten—as they are remembered I will deal with them—*this* is my solemn oath.

---

1. This refers to Kennett Rōshi's first kenshō in Japan.

PLATE VI:– HEAVEN IS THE MOST DANGEROUS OF ALL PLACES.

Absolute blackness; the great darkness of this seeming tunnel is impenetrable. Directly ahead of me is the great, iron pillar, penetrating the universe. From a great distance a bright light flashes, hitting the pillar. This is the road to heaven. I have said no to the abyss, cleansed my heart of its past wrong-doing; I can go into this bright, beautiful light. It flashes on the pillar and descends; each flash is a life as it flies by into heaven. Let me go quickly into this beautiful heaven; let me be there quickly. The flashes grow faster and faster, faster and faster. I am drawn more and more into it; I want to enter it; I want to be there; I want to make an end. I am standing up now. During the past days I have cleansed my spirit. I have searched every part of my heart, torn it to pieces, looked at and rooted out every evil act. During this time I was given the chance to see my past, every day of every year as if in a great mirror, and to deal with what I had done. Daizui has made many 'phone calls and written many letters. The slate is clean. He will take care of that which it is not possible to do at once. I have forgiven all who need to be forgiven as indeed I hope they forgive me. I cannot carry their karma for them; I *must* carry my own; each man his karma makes. So now heaven is my reward; here is the flashing light and soon I will be one of those flashes going into the depth of the great pillar which is the pillar of the universe.

But what is this that I see? This is the same as hell; this is the same as the abyss. The light does not enter the pillar; it goes off into blackness; it flashes, goes out and disappears. I might as well go into the abyss. These are opposites, the abyss and this flashing light. They are the same as all the other opposites; I want no part of them. This is a more dangerous place than the abyss; the flashes seem to radiate truth and beauty but are nothing other than the most dangerous of all opposites. I do not wish to flash into darkness; I do not wish to die for this, indeed, will be *real* death. "Never come too close nor put yourself too far away," —never come too close to heaven lest you be fascinated by it. I halt my steps; the pillar remains silent. The flashing grows slower; the pillar moves aside. Daizui was terrified by the smile on my face. Before me stretches a great, vast blackness...a great, vast blackness....

PLATE VII:— THE VOICE OF THE ETERNAL LORD.

I got up for a few moments this morning and sat in Zazen instead of lying down. I step off into life when my purpose for living emerges. What *is* my purpose for living? Oh, Lord Buddha, teach me! What is my purpose for living? I have cleansed my heart in all the ways I know; I have struggled to find everything that I could possibly have done which would have kept me from knowing the Truth. Oh, Lord Buddha, help me! Show me the way, show me the way. And then, like a flash, a voice said, "What *is* your purpose for living?" With difficulty, for by now I had almost no strength even for speech, my voice falteringly replied, "My purpose is to be a monk."

Then came blessed sleep. Vast emptiness everywhere—vast emptiness. Another day has dawned and the emptiness is vaster than it was before. The blackness is growing lighter but behind me it is absolutely black. My purpose for living is to be a monk; it is sufficient for *me* to be a monk; I need nothing more. I sit again in meditation. What is a monk? I do not know what is a monk. I have been a monk for many years but—what *is* a monk? My kesa[1] is upon my head and the Lord of the House, That which Is, pulls its corner. Yes, indeed, this *is* monkhood—to wear the true kesa of the Lord; true ordination is to *know* what it is to be a monk. But what, indeed, *is* the kesa? What does it mean? What

---

1. The monk's robe.

does it signify? My brain reels. What is it to be a monk? What is the meaning of the kesa? A great lake appears ahead of me—a great and beautiful lake, absolutely still. The moon shines upon it; it is exquisite. Is this, then, to be a monk—to sit still beside the lake, to sit still for eternity? The aloneness is unbelievable—no one, nothing else in sight, no other being, nothing—just alone beside this vast lake with this great moon. Why am I not content?

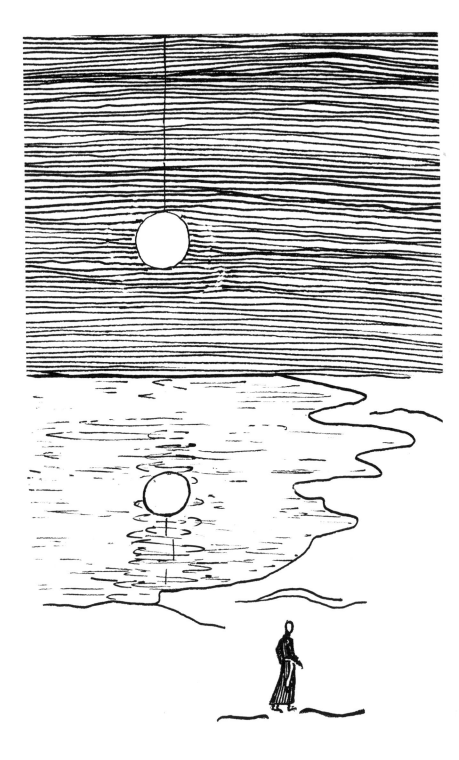

PLATE VIII:– THE LAKE OF QUIETISM.

It is beautiful to sit beside this lake but what is the point? To sit beside a lake looking at a moon for eternity? This is all? I have to find the meaning of the kesa. I must be careful of the training of others but I cannot do it for them. I have made and carried my own karma. They must find their purpose for living as I have found mine. I must know the meaning of the kesa. I have to cross this lake. Behold, the lake has moved aside and the moon is not a moon—it is like a mirror hanging from a string. A voice whispers, "Delusive peace is unmasked. This is the lake of quietism. Here you do *not* stay." If I am to be a live monk I must *know* the harmony of body and mind for the body will not cease from sickness until the mind ceases from evil. To do this I must understand the Precepts absolutely. If I understand them absolutely then I will understand the kesa of the monk and I will indeed be worthy of wearing it. The first Precept is, "Cease from evil."[1] I must know the meaning of "Cease from evil." It sounds so simple but I must know its meaning absolutely. I must look at every fibre of my being and see where evil exists within me. I must clean my passions and, even more, I must clean their impregnations for it is these impregnations that have made me ill, not only in this life but down the centuries. I must know the meaning of "Cease from evil" for this is the house of all the laws of Buddha; this is the source of all the laws of Buddha. The law of karma is one of the five laws of the universe;

---

1. See "Kyojūkaimon" in *Zen is Eternal Life*, p. 266.

it is absolute, it is inescapable. All are bound by the law of karma once it is set in motion. By accident someone made the course of karma; it is not intentionally set in motion; what happens, or happened, or will happen to me or to anyone else is caused by karma; by accident the wheel rolled. Do not continue the rolling of the wheel by dwelling on the past or fearing the future; live now without evil. Stop the wheel *now* by cutting the roots of karma, by knowing the house-builder of the house of ego; if I do not, karma will go on endlessly. The only difference between me and another being is that *I* have the opportunity of knowing the Lord of the House right now, having heard the teachings of the Buddha. Others may have less opportunity than I but, when they hear it, who knows which will be first at the gate of the Treasure House? "Cease from evil" is absolute, in thought, in word, in deed, in body, in spirit. All are bound by the law of karma; do not doubt this. I will pay for everything I do if I do not cut the roots *now* and live by fully-digested, Preceptual Truth. Do not worry about the karma of others; each man his karma makes.

Within me I know that this is the right move for it grows lighter. As I meditate, lying here each day, I take a different Precept and ask That which Is to teach me its meaning. "Do only good," comes next. "The Dharma of Shakyamuni Buddha's Enlightenment is the Dharma of all existence." Do not do anything unless it is 'good;' do not do anything unless I have first asked the Lord of the House if it is good for me to do it. Do nothing whatsoever in a hurry; do nothing whatsoever on the spur of the moment unless I know the *certainty* given by the Lord of the House; know that I must take the consequences of what I do if it is not a fully-digested act for *I* know what lies beyond good and evil, right and wrong; *I* know that which lies beyond morality; I *know* the Lord of the House. Ask the Lord of the House at all times before I do anything whatsoever. "Is it good? Is it your will?" If I do not ask the Lord of the House, the house-builder of the house of ego will again pick up his tools and, before I know it, there will be a great structure from which I cannot escape. If a thing is 'good' in this way it may be done; if it is not 'good' in this way it should not be done; I am not speaking here of good and evil; I am speaking of 'good' in the sense of *if it is right*; this is beyond right and wrong; *if it is good* is beyond good and evil. This teaching is indeed the teaching of Shakyamuni Buddha's enlightenment for there was not one of His acts that was not the result of fully-digested, Preceptual Truth. If I live thus, doing that only which is 'good' after I have asked the Lord of the House, after I *know* the *true* Lord of the House, then I can *know* the teaching of Shakyamuni Buddha's enlightenment and know that His enlightenment and mine are identically the same; but this is only if I know who the Lord of the House is and do not suffer from the idea that *I* am the Lord of the House. Always I must ask the Lord of the House; always I must be humble in His presence. "Please teach me that which it is good for me to do this day. Please show me that which it is good for me to teach this day. Please give me the certainty that I teach the Truth and know, indeed, that, when the still, small voice within my mind and heart says 'Yes,' I must obey that teaching. When it says 'No,' I must *not* disobey that teaching." When the Lord speaks spring up joyfully to answer; then, indeed, it is good to do anything whatsoever; *know* that the Lord will *never* break the Precepts.

The following day comes the last of the Three Pure Precepts—"Do good for others. Be beyond both the holy and the unholy. Let us rescue ourselves and others." Do not set up a chain of causation that will cause others to do wrong; do not do that which will cause another to grieve; do not do that which will result in my creating karma for another being; do not accidentally set the wheel of karma in motion. Do not let myself hear the words, "What demon allowed you to become a priest? From what demon did you learn Buddhism?" To be beyond both the holy and the unholy, to be beyond praise and blame, to act only from what the Lord of the House teaches without worrying whatsoever what the world may think is indeed to have understood the Three Pure Precepts. Before any act is performed I must ask myself, "Am I ceasing from evil in doing this act? Is it good in the sight of the Lord of the House? Shall I cause another being to do harm either to himself or to others? I cannot stop *him* doing harm, for each man his karma makes and must carry for himself, but I can do that about myself which will prevent *me* from accidentally starting the course of karma. I must think carefully of my every act. I may not cause another to make a mistake in Buddhism." By so doing I rescue both myself and others for, in cutting the roots of karma for myself, I cut the roots of karma for others also. These three are called the Three Pure Precepts. Without them I cannot live the Buddhist life.

And now I am truly given the hossu for I have the right to use it. When it is moved from left to right and then again to the left the Three Pure Precepts are shown; as I hold it high so they may be seen in the world in my actions; according as it is held so the Precepts may be seen. This is the beginning of the meaning of the kesa. Each day, after this, one of the Precepts is given and, each day, I meditate upon it. So, in all, for sixteen days, I study the Precepts thus and I write them here.

"Do not kill. No life can be cut off for the Life of Buddha is increasing. Continue the life of Buddha and do not kill Buddha." Above all, do not turn my face away from Buddha, the Lord of the House, for this is indeed to commit spiritual suicide; to kill Buddha is to turn away from Buddha. "Man stands in his own shadow and wonders why it is dark yet only he can turn round." To turn away from Buddha is to say, "My ego is greater than the Lord of the House; my opinions are more right; my wishes are more important." It is *I* whom I kill. If I do not listen to the Lord of the House in this life in what life will I listen to the Lord of the House? Will I for eternity attempt to commit *real* suicide? If I always face the Buddha I will always know Buddha; if I always listen to the Lord of the House there is no possibility of my ever killing anything.

"Do not steal. The mind and its object are one. The gateway to enlightenment stands open wide." But there is nothing whatsoever that can be stolen. "Now you have, so guard well," says the scripture; each of us possesses the Treasure House. All we have to do is ask the Dragon for permission to enter, ask the Dragon if we may see the jewel and it will be given to us. He who tries to rob himself, he who tries to steal from the Treasure House can never have the Treasure; erudition is as this; taking drugs is as this. All I have to do is ask the Lord of the House and I may know and possess all things. The gateway to enlightenment does indeed stand open wide for the true mind of the Buddha and the jewel are one and the same; ask the Lord of the House at all times and the gates will be thrown wide open. Remember that he who counts another's treasure can never have his own; he who steals can only ever rob himself.

"Do not covet. The doer, the doing and that which has the doing done to it are immaculate, therefore there is no desire. It is the same doing as that of the Buddhas." Thus there is nothing to be coveted and no one that covets. "Now you *have*, so guard well," says the scripture.[2] Since there is nothing from the first, how can there be anything to guard well? "The white snow falls upon the silver plate; the snowy heron in the bright moon hides. Resembles each the other yet these two are not the same."[3] Thus we think there is a difference; thus we think there is an ability to covet and something *to* covet; thus man makes mistakes. Indeed there *is* nothing from the first.

"Do not say that which is not true. The wheel of the Dharma rolls constantly and lacks for nothing yet needs something." The Dharma is Truth itself but it needs expression. He who lies does not allow the Dharma to show itself, he does not allow the Dharma to be expressed, he does not allow the world to *see* the Dharma Wheel in action. "And still the sweet dew covers the whole world, including those who lie, and within that dew lies the Truth."

"Do not sell the wine of delusion. But there is nothing to be deluded about. If we realise this we are enlightenment itself." "Thus shall ye think of all this fleeting world, a star at dawn, a bubble in a stream, a child's laugh, a phantasm, a dream."[4] If I hold on to nothing whatsoever there can be no delusion nor can

---

2. From the Zen Scripture, Hōkyozammai.

3. Ibid.

4. Taken from *The Diamond Scripture*, section 32. See *The Diamond Sutra and The Sutra of Hui Neng*, Trans. A. F. Price and Wong Mou-Lam, Shambhala, 1969.

there be enlightenment; then there are no opposites. Thus, indeed, we are enlightenment itself—yet always we will have the form and figure of old monks.

"Do not speak against others." Do not speak against the Lord of the House. Every person, every being *is* the Temple of the Lord wherein the Lord dwells, the still water wherein the Dragon lives. If I speak against others I speak against the Lord of the House. Do not try to divide the Lord of the House; do not try to cause war within the Lord; do not try to make the Lord make war upon Himself. "In Buddhism, the Truth and everything are the same; the same law, the same enlightenment and the same behaviour. Do not allow any one to speak of another's faults." Do not find fault with the Lord of the House. "Do not allow any one to make a mistake in Buddhism." To speak against the Lord of the House is the gravest mistake of which I know.

"Do not be proud of yourself and devalue others." It is enough for me to *know* the Lord of the House, to know that He dwells within all things. How can there be devaluation of others if they are the Temple of the Lord? How can there be pride if all possess equally within the Lord? "Every Buddha and every Ancestor realises that he is the same as the limitless sky and as great as the universe. When they realise their true body there is nothing within or without; when they realise their true body they are nowhere more upon the earth." There is nothing to be proud of and nothing to be devalued.

"Do not be mean in giving either Dharma or wealth." Since all possess the Lord, there is nothing to be given and nothing to be taken away, and yet all things must be given, all things offered at all times and in all places. "One phrase, one verse, the hundred grasses,"—all contain the Lord, all express the Lord—

each in its own way and each perfectly. "One Dharma, one enlightenment, every Buddha, every Ancestor." No difference, nothing greater, nothing smaller; nothing truer, nothing less true. When all is within the Lord, all stand straight together, a million Buddhas stand in one straight line. Out of gratitude to the Buddhas and Patriarchs I give Dharma, I give wealth, I give life itself—strength, youth, beauty, wealth, everything that I have and, even then, I cannot give thanks enough for one second of their true training; I can never repay their kindness to me. Only by my own true training is this possible and then, again, there is no repayment; it is just the work of a Buddha.

"Do not be angry. There is no retiring, no going, no Truth, no lie; there is a brilliant sea of clouds, there is a dignified sea of clouds." Just there is that going on which causes me to see unclearly; but if I truly look, if I look with care, I will see that the true and beautiful sky is shining behind the clouds; I may see the Lord of the House. No matter how angry the person is who is with me, I may see in him, too, the Lord if I am truly looking, if my own ego is out of the way and, in seeing the Lord in him, he can see the Lord in me. The depth of the ocean is still even when there is a great storm upon its surface; thus should I be when there is anger, knowing that nothing whatsoever can touch the Truth.

"Do not defame the Three Treasures. To do something by ourselves, without copying others, is to become an example to the world and the merit of doing such a thing becomes the source of all wisdom. Do not criticise but accept everything." The Lord of the House does not do things in the normally accepted ways, nor do the Buddhas and Patriarchs; they are not individual and they are not the same as each other. Each expresses the Truth in his own way as do all things; they do that which is their way and express the

Lord within it. Do not criticise the way of another, do not call it into question; look within it and see the Lord. Look with the mind of a Buddha and I will see the heart of a Buddha. To criticise is to defame the Lord of the House. Love the Lord of the House at all times—know Him, talk to Him; never let a day go by when I do not consult with Him even on the slightest matter. Then I will never, as long as I live, defame the Three Treasures.

Above all, the Precepts "Do not kill" and "Do not steal" seem to stand out as did the first Three. Then comes the day of "What is Buddha? What is Dharma? And what is Sangha?" "In the Three Treasures of Buddha, Dharma and Sangha there are three merits. The first is the true source of the Three Treasures;"—there *is* an unborn, uncreated, unformed, undying, indestructible, the Lord of the House, That which speaks in silence and in stillness, the "still, small voice."

"The second merit is the presence in the past of Shakyamuni Buddha"—all those who have truly transmitted Buddhism throughout eternity.

"The third is His presence at the present time,"—all those who transmit the Truth, who live by the Precepts and make them their blood and bones, the embodiment of the Preceptual Truth of the Buddhas.

"The highest Truth is called the Buddha Treasure,"—the knowledge of that which is, the knowledge of the unformed, uncreated, unborn, undying, indestructible; the certainty, without doubt, of its existence, the *knowledge* of it within oneself, the Buddha *living* within oneself, the Lord of the House who directs all things. If I study true Buddhism I will become as the water wherein the Dragon dwells; it is necessary to know the true Dragon; it is necessary to ask the Dragon, the Lord of the House, at all times to help and to teach.

Only if I give all that is required of the price that the Dragon asks will he show me the jewel; I must accept the jewel from the Dragon without doubting its value or querying the price. "Immaculacy is called the Dharma Treasure,"— one must live with the roots of karma cut away. To do this I must indeed know the house-builder of this house of ego, know all his tools, know all his building materials; there is no other way that I can know immaculacy. The house-builder of the house of ego must be known absolutely, recognised at all times. It is not enough to have a kenshō; I must go back to the source of the karmic stream; I must return to that source to find out what set it going. Kenshō wipes the slate clean; to find the source of karma cuts its roots and, with constant training, keeps the slate clean but, since there is nothing from the first, there is nothing clean and nothing that is unclean—I cannot know this, however, until I have first tried to clean it. "Most houses can do with a thorough sweeping but even a million sweepings will not clear away the dust completely." Thus I remain in my body and accept it, knowing that *nothing matters*, that I am immaculate, always was and always will be. This is the immaculacy of the Dharma Treasure; this makes the immaculacy and harmony of the Sangha Treasure possible. It is the knowledge of the True Kesa, that which is immaculate above all dust and dirt, the knowledge that the dust and dirt are indeed a figment of my own imagination as a result of past, accrued karma, that makes possible the Transmission of the Light from the far past to the now and the far future without words. The scriptures show up blank pages; there *is* a Transmission that lies beyond them.

"Harmony is the Sangha Treasure"—this is brought about by the knowledge that, no matter what I, a member of the Sangha, may do, I *am* immaculate from the very beginning; there *is* nothing from the first. "Thus shall ye think of all this fleeting world, a star at dawn, a bubble in a stream, a child's laugh, a phantasm, a dream." Although this is true I, the members of the Sangha, the Zen Masters, all beings are bound by the law of karma; we will pay the price of what we do. Thus is the mind of the Sangha Treasure.

"The person who has realised the Truth really is called the Buddha Treasure;"–he *is* the embodiment of the Truth, he *is* Nirvana, he *is* the Embodiment of Enlightenment, he *is* the Treasure of the Buddha for, in him, can be seen fully-digested, Preceptual Truth.

"The Truth that is realised by Buddha is called the Dharma Treasure,"–that is the *knowledge* of the unborn, uncreated, unformed, undying, indestructible; the living with this knowledge without doubt, the trusting eternally of the Lord of the House, the certainty of the Treasure House within me at the gate of which sits the True Dragon Who *is* indeed the Lord of the House.

"The people who study that which lies within the Treasure House are called the Treasure of the Sangha,"–the Dharma and the Sangha are one and the same thing, being the embodiment each of the other if fully-digested, Preceptual Truth is their rule of life. When I ask, 'What is a monk?' I *know* that it is my Kesa.

"He who teaches devas and humans is called the Buddha Treasure,"–only if I give true teaching, being beyond praise and blame, the holy and the unholy, right and wrong, without fear or favor, if I become 'good' for others.

"That which appears in the world in the scriptures and is 'good' for others is called the Dharma Treasure,"–anything may teach. However infinitesimally small, however large, no matter what, all things may teach the Dharma when they live by fully-digested, Preceptual Truth, when they have cut away the roots of karma, when they know the house-builder of the house of ego and are constantly keeping him from rebuilding again as a result of *practising* fully-digested, Preceptual Truth.

"He who is released from all suffering and is beyond the world is called the Sangha Treasure;"—he for whom no longer desires burn, wherein wants and cravings no longer exist; he who gets up in the morning and goes to sleep at night, eats when he is hungry, sleeps when he is tired, is satisfied with that which he is given and does not ask for more than he can absolutely use in the immediate now. When someone is converted to the Three Treasures thus, he can have the Precepts of the Buddhas absolutely.

In this manner I make the True Buddha my teacher and do not follow wrong ways. The True Buddha that is my Teacher is indeed the Lord of the House, the True Dragon. Do not hold on to my tiny kenshō; trust the Lord of the House, hold fast by Him no matter what state I may be in, whether I am well or sick, brightly alive or dying, hold fast by the Lord of the House.

And, with each Precept, comes a different symbol of the priesthood. It is as if I am given each symbol as I understand each Precept and I hold it reverently and place it upon the altar of my heart.

PLATE IX:– VAST EMPTINESS.

The land is less arid and beginning to turn green. As I go on my journey the Lord of the House, That which Is, says, "As you wish," whenever I make my decisions; the consequences are not His problem; they are mine. I study the scriptures line by line but, above all, come the words, "Never come too close nor put yourself too far away." "I have torn my life to shreds. What more is required of me, Oh Lord of the House? Tell me and I will do it. I will not disobey Your will." For eight months I have been under attack–from sickness, from worldly affairs and those who would assail the spirit and prevent its growth.

For some few days now Daizui and I have been noticing differences in our appearance in fleeting glances. Since I have cleaned and purified my karma of this life it is now necessary to clean the impregnations that the karma of my past lives has left upon my skhandas. This is one of the deeper meanings of the second Noble Truth of the Buddha, suffering's cause; to this end we are both noticing these differences. He looks at me and for a fleeting moment sees a very old European Christian monk; he is very happy, he has left behind no unclean impregnations. Behind him is a Chinese Buddhist monk; he too is happy with nothing unclean left behind. Further and further back I go. An old Japanese monk is seen with bushy eyebrows and a stern expression but he, too, has left no trace behind him. Behind him stands a fierce Tartar but he is clean – and weaving in and out between them all is a sad and beautiful woman from the late eighteen-hundreds.

Her eyes do not show the peace that do the eyes of the others. Here is something with which I must deal. "Oh, unhappy woman, you are not me; all that is left of you is with me. Let me know what you have done; let me understand what causes you to still be so sad." Before me I see her actions and understand the confusion she felt at her death. I recognise in me the impregnations these actions have left and resolve to be aware of, and learn from, her mistakes for my skhandas possess tiny seeds which may be germinated by the karma of former lives. When I purify this karma these seeds cannot germinate. This woman was religious and, when dying in a foreign country, longed to hear the absolution of her sins in her mother tongue but no priest who spoke it could be found. To bring her peace I recite the absolution for her but some confusion over past acts still remains for Christian doctrine does not well understand the Law of Karma. "I will do what I can to ease your mind. I embrace you. You must forgive all those who wronged or harmed you and you must take refuge in the Buddha, refuge in the Dharma, refuge in the Sangha. Because of your ignorance of the Four Noble Truths of the Lord of the House, the existence of suffering, suffering's cause, the cessation of suffering and the Noble Eightfold Path, you performed acts which had horrible results. If you had known these Truths you would have understood the Law of Karma which teaches that every cause has an effect and you would not have committed these acts. Because of your ignorance and confusion concerning this at the time of your death, what had been your karma caused me to come into existence. The purpose of my life until now has been the conversion of your ignorance. Now that this conversion has been accomplished the root of your karma has been cut and the time of repayment is over. This conversion is acknowledged by the Lord of the House and witnessed by this pure-hearted congregation. By the guidance of the Buddhas and Patriarchs you have discarded and purified all your karma of body, mouth and will and obtained great immaculacy. This is by the power of conversion. The purpose of our life in the future is the good of all beings. I do not turn away from you. Let us, together with all beings, take Refuge in the Buddha, Refuge in the Dharma, Refuge in the Sangha. You should know that 'only volition is the doer of karma, and only feeling is the reaper of karma. In the ultimate sense,

> No doer is there who does the deed,
> Nor is there one who feels the fruit.' "[1]

Her eyes are now clear and pure and full of joy; a great peace descends. This is the end of past karma on the human plane. Down the centuries I have been a monk so many times; fifteen times Christian, fourteen Buddhist, sometimes male, sometimes female. Now must come the karma from lives in the formless realms and from animal lives; it is my duty to go on. *All* that which I did in past lives, in all worlds, all must be cleansed away before I can become one with the Eternal Lord.

Upon the formless plane once there raged a great battle wherein I was gravely injured; unto this day I bear the psychic wounds. These must be healed by those who inflicted them not because they will not heal of themselves but because I must give an opportunity to convert themselves from their former evil to those who caused them. This I have done. One key life, that of a great white tiger, still remains to be seen but this is not yet to be. The hordes of Mara,—I hear them, I hear them. My resolve is strong, I will not flinch. This I *know* and go on unafraid for, if there is fear, then there

---

1. *Manual of Buddhism*, Narada Thera.

is no way of becoming one with the Lord. Always read the "Sandōkai," always read the "Hōkyozammai," always read "The Scripture of Great Wisdom,"—they guard and teach so well. If I am to be a monk I must unceasingly heed the Lord of the House. When the Lord of the House gives me His teaching, when He gives me His requests, His orders, listen attentively and respectfully and, quickly, loudly, reverently and obediently say, "*YES.*" Never query the Lord of the House even if He sends me into battle with the army of Mara; go gladly and willingly, knowing that I cannot be harmed by Mara; go quickly; go obediently.

PLATE X:– THE ARMY OF MARA.

The physical illness is now over and I returned to Shasta a week ago but I am still weak and so friends help in dealing with Mara. His attack was timed to coincide with my regaining my health. I *know* that I cannot be harmed but the kindness of others is very great; surrounded by them Mara's demons may try to attack but they cannot enter the circle. All is safe within. First comes sweet sleep; be watchful, be aware. Then comes wan doubt, then fear, then greed for sex and food and all the things the world calls good; ghastly haunted faces, fearful to behold. Weak from illness, lack of food and sleep though I may be, you shall not prevail against me. I *will* meet the Lord face to face. I must have compassion for, and convert, these hordes of Mara. "You, take refuge in the Buddha; You, take refuge in the Dharma; You, take refuge in the Sangha. Because of your ignorance of the Four Noble Truths of the Lord of the House, the existence of suffering, suffering's cause, the cessation of suffering and the Noble Eightfold Path, you caused acts which had horrible results. If you had known these Truths you would have understood the Law of Karma which teaches that every cause has an effect and you would not have caused these acts for you yourself *are* Buddha. You already have all the aspects of a Buddha in your own way; you do not need to steal from yourself. The Body of the Lord of the House permeates the universe and manifests Itself in everything; there is no being, thing or force in which It does not so manifest Itself. It does so for every relationship and in all need; but, to do so, It has to be still in Its *own* true place. *Your* true place is not here with men. You *will* return to your rightful place where indeed you *are* a beautiful Buddha. There the seas of your merit cannot be counted. We pray that the Three Treasures may give all of us their loving kindness. We have offered many things that exist within the sea, the fields and the mountains and opened the Gate of the Dharma that is the most excellent in all the world. We pray that the merit thereof may be turned to the good of you and all things in the endless worlds, to the spirits that are lacking in wealth in the nether worlds and to the evil and wicked in heaven. We pray that everything may realise the Truth and be released from all bad karma born of body, mouth and will, make the hidden and apparent free and complete the Right and True Wisdom. We love you, we do not turn away from you.

Homage to all Buddhas in all worlds,
Homage to all the Bodhisattvas in all worlds,
Homage to the Scripture of Great Wisdom."

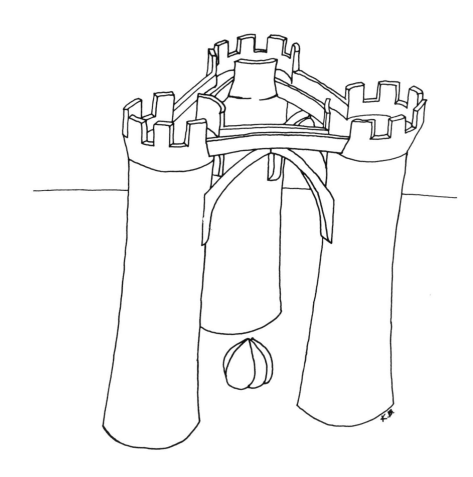

PLATE XI:— THE APPEARANCE OF THE MANDALA.

There is a great waveless sea that I see dimly. Within its centre is a lotus bud surrounded by three towers. I do not know the meaning; I cannot comprehend it.

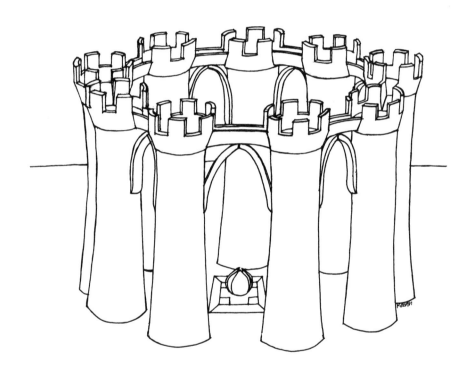

PLATE XII:– THE GROWING MANDALA.

The mandala now has nine towers; between each tower is an arch spanned by battlements. Within the centre of the mandala is a haiseki and, upon it, is a lotus bud. The water laps up to the edge of the steps but it does not come over them onto the floor or the haiseki. There is great stillness. A monk sits still upon each tower in meditation, so very still...the stillness that comes before the dawn.

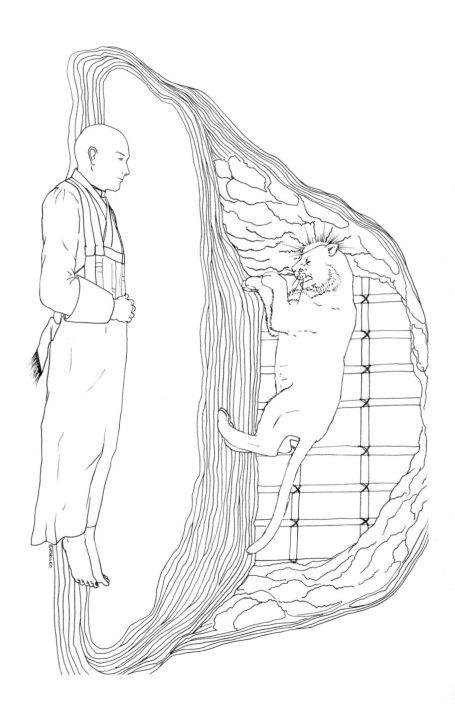

GYOKUKO

PLATE XIII:– THE SOURCE OF THE KŌAN.

It is the 25th. of October. I am well now but still weak. This morning I experienced living absolutely a life in which, three thousand years ago, I had been a white tiger, captured whilst eating a heron, by a tribe of Indians whose religious cult was one of tiger worship. The tiger loved the greenery of the open air; it was young, full of the joy of life and would not accept its captivity. Constantly pacing back and forth, back and forth, bashing its head against the bars and walls of its cage, it gave itself a stroke. The despair of the animal was intense; I found it overwhelming. Its longing for freedom and the open sky echoes through every fibre of me as clearly as it did three thousand years ago. Its grief is my grief; its longing my longing; its pain my pain. For years I have had weakness in my legs and now I know why. By giving itself a stroke the tiger had paralysed its hind legs and this was made worse by a blow on the head from one of its captors. I can feel the uselessness in my own thighs and understand fully the skhandic memory that has come down the centuries in that part of my body. In every life since the tiger's my legs have been weak. The despair that came in Sōji-ji, when people made it so difficult for me to be the true monk I wanted to be, caused me to begin to limp; I now know the source of this. "Oh sweet tiger, dying in this dungeon hole, all you ever wanted to be was a tiger, nothing more, but these men, in their ignorance, thought you had power. They wanted it from you and so destroyed your youth and life. You just wanted to be you, the you you knew you were; you had no wish to be a god. Now indeed I know the source of my kōan and why my legs have retained the memory of your pain, for all my life I have wanted to be a simple monk; high places and great names are not for me and yet the world has denied me this right. When I at last went to the east no one would believe that this was all I asked. And so the reporters came in droves to interview and photograph and I was sent here and there to be stared at and discussed and, all the time, my heart bled for all *I* wished was to *be* a monk—and all *you* wished was to *be* a tiger. You could no more understand why they should want you than I could understand why my family and the reporters did what they did. For us it was so very simple; we wanted to be what we knew we were and not be made over into what others wanted us to be. I can remember the weakness in my legs increasing terribly when I was at school and going away somewhat after I left; that school had only one aim—to turn me into what I was not—a high-born lady. From henceforth you and I will be ourselves; I do not want your power; if I could give you back your life I would but I am not able. You misunderstood where true freedom was to be found at the time of your death because these silly men tried to make you a god—know that true freedom lies within. I was once a woman named Alexia; she too had weakness in her legs; she too believed she was not free and so helped cause a revolution. Your story and hers are identical in their mistakes but hers were greater for she was human. She is at rest now and you and I will be at rest when we forgive the ignorance of those who caused our grief. You must forgive your captors as I forgive those who would not let me be a monk as I had understood it. After all, the only true monk lies within. I love you so very much; more than anything I have ever loved in my entire life. It does not matter if the strength never returns to my

67

legs—keep it, dear tiger, for it is yours. For a moment you doubted your true nature long ago and so caused the karmic memory that lies within me. We will never doubt again and so the time of wandering is over, our cage has disappeared." And I loved the tiger as I have never loved anything in my entire life and, for the first time, experienced being loved in return.

So, accepting fully the sadness and grief of this tiger, I lay still and it lay down upon my breast, its body along mine. I feel its tail in my right knee; I know the feel of fur upon my face and left hand. As I walk I feel the strength that it once possessed in my legs and long to bound as it did long ago.

For twenty-four hours I have been living in the oneness of love with my tiger. However, when asking the Eternal Lord what I should do next, I discover that Mara is using my love just as he uses everything else. I have known so little love; it has been so exquisite—but there is danger in loving too much. So, in great grief, I pluck the tiger from my breast, ordain it and celebrate Segaki—it does not need the latter but it is good to do the ceremony.

PLATE XIV:— APPEARANCE IN THE HALL OF SHADOWS.

I have known love for so short a time; something has to be done—I must accept the tiger back into me and not discard it. How can this be done? I know the way. I must open myself completely to the tiger whilst saying no to Mara. I open my left hand, holding the manji within it, saying, "Come, enter me, all that is good within this tiger; but anything that is not of the Eternal Lord must stay outside." I feel energy enter my left arm; I know that the tiger has entered me. It curls up within my hara, grows smaller and smaller, is now a tiny dot. But what is this? The dot, as it vanishes, is becoming something else—a beautiful, golden thing, like a golden Buddha; not quite triangular, more teardrop shaped; old gold in colour; it is an exquisite thing to have within me. It sits in shadow, as if in an unillumined hall the walls of which I know to be white and purple.

PLATES XV AND XVI:— THE SPIRIT RISES TO GREET THE LORD.

For the rest of that day I was in very deep meditation. It is now the morning of the 28th. and I am lying in bed, having just awakened. I am conscious of the fact that the golden Buddha within me is moving; it seems to be going upwards. It reaches my throat, goes up the back of my head and sits on top of it. From there it moves to the front where it leaves a mark upon my forehead; I feel it to be the mark of a small Buddha; as if someone has imprinted a tiny Buddha there. But there is also something left outside on top of my head. After the mark has been imprinted, that which first moved moves on, going within me through the mark on my forehead, down the front of me, and again stays in my hara which, from having been dark the day before, now seems to be filled with white light. I know that there is something that I need to hear; I do not know what it is. I know that absolute stillness is necessary. There are four other monks in the room besides Daizui:— Sanshō, Kyogen, Jitsudō and Ekō. It is almost as though I do not want them to breathe for the slightest sound should not be heard.

PLATES XVII, XVIII AND XIX:— STRUCK BY THE SWORD OF BUDDHA'S WISDOM.

Everything in my body is absolutely still, nothing stirs within or without. I know that I have to hear something but I do not know what. Daizui, in deep meditation, says that it has something to do with, "Within these Precepts dwell the Buddhas." I immediately remember that this is part of the *Shushōgi*[1] but give the wrong page thinking it is the end of the fourth chapter instead of the end of the third. Jitsudō, however, knows what I mean and reads the following:—

> Within these Precepts dwell the Buddhas, enfolding all things within their unparallelled wisdom. There is no distinction between subject and object for any who dwell herein. All things, earth, trees, wooden posts, bricks, stones, become Buddhas once this refuge is taken. From these Precepts come forth such a wind and fire that all are driven into enlightenment when the flames are fanned by the Buddha's influence. This is the merit of non-action and non-seeking; the awakening to True Wisdom.

At the word "awakening" something strikes me on the forehead where is the mark. It strikes with such force I gasp—in amazement? acceptance? I cannot tell you what has happened but Daizui knows that, for a moment, I died. My whole body is flooded with something; my hands are open in a gesture of wonder and

---

1. See *Zen is Eternal Life*, pp. 154-163.

amazement—I do not know if wonder is the right word—just amazement and acceptance: My head pains considerably from the blow for, indeed, it is a blow from the Sword of Buddha's Wisdom. With it something opens in the centre of my forehead, where the mark is, and into it streams yellow light. For a long time I lay very still and then it is over. I am conscious of the fact that there seems to be something upon my head and I know that it is like a lotus blossom crown; I know too that there is something above my head. Daizui says he sees what seems to be a bud on a silver stem. At the time of being struck I asked the others what they saw. Kyogen saw a great, silver sea and, within it, a bright light that he knew was my body. Ekō saw a great, silver and green lotus floating above high mountains.

Daizui looks at what he thought was the bud this evening and sees that it has the shape of a silvery blob on a silver stalk. He sees no colours. Jitsudō says that it looks like a pink bud in the centre of a crown of pink and indigo. That which is on my forehead feels like a small, flattened statue of Buddha and, within it, is a round, glass-like jewel—I cannot fully describe it; I can see it on my forehead but no words come out accurately. I am conscious of being in a great lake.

I am conscious of the bud on my head and can see the crown when I look upwards. It is as though I can see the top of my head and that which is on my forehead; I almost never look down—always up.

PLATE XX:– THE TIME OF SEGAKI.

Today we celebrated the great Segaki of Obon which we now hold on the 31st. of October. It was held on the platform that is the foundation for the new Hondō; we gave the merit to all the poor beings who have waited for so many centuries to be free. Many of the monks here have been working in order to see the existence of suffering and its cause in themselves and, in the course of so doing, have seen their past lives as in a mirror showing them the suffering they have caused down the centuries quite clearly. Although they have inherited the same karmic stream as the beings they once were they nevertheless are *not* those same beings; hence the necessity of a Segaki for them. This is a difficult point for some people to understand but it is very important to remember that there is no such thing as an immortal soul or ego that passes from life to life; to quieten the jangles in the karmic stream is one thing; to believe that you *are* those jangles is quite another. To do such a thing would be to become possessed. This is one meaning of the scriptural line, "You are not him;" however, what *he* did does affect *you* until you have either paid in full for, or converted by seeing the cause of the stream of karmic suffering, that which he did. Thus the Christian Bible rightly states, "The sins of the fathers shall be visited on the children to the third and fourth generation of them that hate me"–except that it usually seems to take a lot more than three or four generations to clean up the karmic stream completely enough to again become one with the Lord of the House. I have never before in my life been so joyful when doing a ceremony nor have I ever held my head so high without pride. I am a priest.

When I woke up this morning I knew that I was in a lotus pool and that, on either side of me, were lotus blossoms that were anxious to look at me; it was as if they had come for greeting. It is very beautiful; they stayed with me all day and are with me still.

PLATES XXI AND XXII:– RECOGNITION IN THE WAVELESS SEA.

It is the morning of the lst. of November, Founder's Day. I intend to go to meditation but it becomes very obviously unwise to do so in the formal sense. I am aware of a group of beings coming to meet me; in some way I am to be greeted. Within the centre of them is a magnificent, golden being; it leans down and it touches me. Now I seem to be standing away from the group and seeing myself being embraced; I know that I want to speak to it. I do not know what to say so I ask, "May I look at you?" I am then enfolded in gold, in this beautiful golden–I cannot find the right words; my entire body is thrilled through and through with an energy and a life, a luminescent water of the spirit. It is as if I am bathed within warm, golden light. This happened as I tried to raise my eyes to look at it; I had only lifted them a little when this happened. I stay thus for a long time. Then I feel it recede with the whole group and I find myself seated in a lotus blossom looking at an immense sea–an incredibly large, waveless sea. From one end to the other it is *full* of lotus blossoms just like mine, millions upon millions, and yet it is not overcrowded; the sky is exquisite– light shimmering where the water meets the pale, blue sky. I am conscious of a group at a distance on the shore. I ask what I should do and am told to celebrate the ceremony for Founder's Day; I rise to do so imme- diately upon hearing the Lord's will although I have been dead, it would seem, for a short time. I get up with incredible energy and do the Founder's Ceremony on the new Hondō foundations. Upon my return to my room I ask what to do next and I am told to stay in my lotus. I spend the day just sitting here loving the sea, drinking in its beauty, its radiance and its peace. Evening wears on, night falls; light shimmers on the horizon where the sea meets the dark, velvety sky full of exquisite stars and a great moon. On the shore are shadowy buildings; the lotus blossoms are closing. I do not want to go to sleep; I do not want my bloom to close. I am conscious of the fact that something is a little worried about this for I should have closed my bloom at sundown as did the others. I stay up very late. There is still pain in my forehead at the spot where I was struck.

It is the morning of the 2nd. of November. I awaken upon the shore; it is very dark. I hear the dawn drum—there is a dawn drum here as at Shasta—and I look up and see beings trooping down to the water's edge to sit in their lotus blossoms. I do not want to leave the shore; I want to stay; I want to stay here so much. And something comes and very gently shoos me off the shore into my blossom and I sit in it and look around me. I see that several of the blossoms have rings of towers around them.

Then the water seems to evaporate and I am back on the haiseki; the towers are around me and I know they are the monks. I do not want to stay down here; I want to get back up as fast as I can; I want to get back to the surface of the lake. But I must understand why the sea evaporated. I must know that here in Shasta is the Buddha Land; as above so below. If I do not make the Buddha Land appear for those around me I am unfit to be a priest. Each of these exquisite creatures, these monks of Shasta, is as a precious jewel given into my keeping by the Lord of the House to guard and to polish. However much I wish to sit above in the beauty and the stillness it must be my pleasure and my joy to bring them, should they so wish, to this blissful place that they may meet their True Lord. My duty from hereon is the harmonisation of heaven and earth. This is the meaning of the first line of the Bodhisattva vow: — However innumerable beings are I vow to save them endlessly. The meditation hall of Shasta is the waveless sea and I have failed in my duty to the Lord if all here do not realise that this monastery *is* indeed the Buddha Land.

I am told that I can go back to the shore at night. I must confess I can hardly wait for the night to come. Perhaps there is still some clinging in me; I must watch this tendency.

PLATE XXIII: – THE LORD'S WILL.

It is the morning of the 3rd. of November. I awaken early and want to get back quickly to a meditation place on the shores of the lake rather than in the sea but I find I am to assist the Lord of the House. I know that I cannot go deeply into meditation until Daizui is in the room; for some reason the Lord needs him here. The ceiling begins to go yellow, as is usual when I enter these meditations, and I seem to be looking out of the place in the centre of my forehead. I see myself on the left hand of a being whom I know to be Shakyamuni Buddha dressed in white; I am holding a canopy over a small and beautiful being seated in a golden lotus that is being held by two other beings like myself. I can feel the lotus crown upon my head and I know that there is a halo behind it. Shakyamuni Buddha bends forward and takes the little being into his arms. For a long time he embraces it; then he straightens up and the golden lotus goes, of itself, back to the sea; the little being is placed in his newly-opened lotus blossom.

We turn and follow Shakyamuni Buddha into one of the huge, shadowy temples that are here but we only go just within the door whilst he goes inside. I want to go inside too but know that I should not; the other beings who are with me troop back to the shore and enter their lotus blossoms. I linger on the shore; I do not want to go. I turn and look back and Shakyamuni Buddha is outside the temple; he waves to me. I go to my lotus blossom and, as I look back at the shore, I see him rise up from where he is standing and become absorbed into the great, golden Cosmic Buddha that I now see in the sky. He is taken into the Cosmic Buddha and yet is separate from Him. He is not the Cosmic Buddha but there is nothing in him that is not of the Cosmic Buddha; the two are inseparable and different. I ask what I should do for this day—should I wish to stay in this heavenly place or is there something else that the Eternal Lord wishes. I am told that, for this day, I should sit within my lotus blossom and meditate until I am needed to do something else; this is what I am doing. The white figure descends from the sky and enters the mark on my forehead; I feel Him within my hara. Daizui saw part of this today.

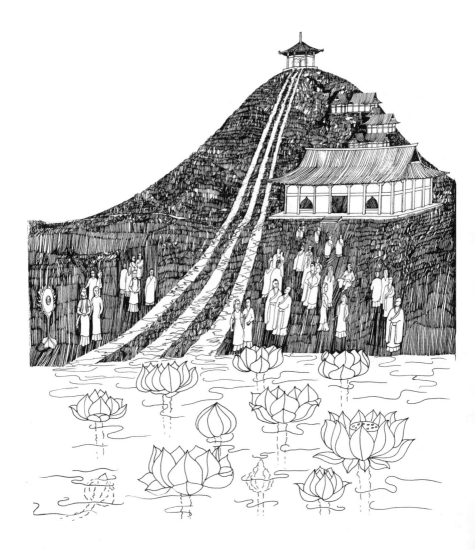

PLATE XXIV:– DO NOT STAY IN HEAVEN.

It is the same evening and we are celebrating Nenju. As each of the names of the Ten Buddhas is recited they appear before me. Now I know why the Holy Lotus Scripture is included as one of the Ten Buddhas; it refers to the waveless sea that is filled with all beings on their lotus thrones. When I first started experiencing these things a little while ago I became frightened lest I be caught up in the experience but the warning against seeing Buddhas or demons is very specific; it is only dangerous to see them when you *feel elation or fear or cling to them*. If I remain unattached to these experiences all will be well. Because I almost made this mistake the sea and the lotuses were less vivid towards the end of today and this worried me. When Daizui asked the Lord the reason he was told that to see them vividly all the time did not make for strong stems on the lotus blossoms. I understand the Lord's words and am grateful for this teaching. The root of the lotus is in the world as we know it; accordingly as we train ourselves so the stem of the lotus pushes upward towards the surface of the sea; if the stem is weak or becomes broken the blossom will die. What a precious teaching this is; in all worlds the human is the highest life.

It is the morning of the 4th. of November and everything is very clear and bright again; not quite as clear as on that first day but the colours are still very vivid, the beings are strolling about in highly-coloured clothing. I climb to the top of a very beautiful, grassy hill behind the main temple and just sit there enjoying myself. There is a spring caught as a fountain on top of the hill under a pavilion. Sometimes the water in the fountain flows down the hill in streams across the green grass to the sea; and then again the streams dry up and steam gently in the sun leaving the grass brighter. Just sitting here I say to myself, "What shall I do today? Nobody seems to be going to the temple at all. There is a ceremony here in Shasta; maybe there shouldn't be one. I will go to the temple anyway." I go into the temple and there is a huge statue of what I have seen in the sky; the Cosmic Buddha with Shakyamuni beside Him. I just sit down on the floor—no one else seems to be here but this does not matter. My eyes insist on closing—I do not dare to look; something comes and holds me and then passes on. When I can open my eyes again I see that Shakyamuni is embracing a shadowy figure further on; there are other shadowy figures in the hall. I go outside the temple and sit by the sea, putting my toes in it.

There are a lot of buds coming up in the sea and one of them I know is one of the monks here; I am told which one but I may not tell him; it is a green bud. I think for a moment Mara has ensnared me, for I have never before seen a boat on the waveless sea, but it is Shakyamuni and some of the beings inspecting the new buds; the one belonging to the monk here is about four inches below the water; it is *very* green. Shakyamuni looks down, saying, "Um." He is very interested in his buds. He returns to the shore in his boat.

I might as well go to Morning Service here in Shasta so I go. We are reciting the names of the Buddhas and Patriarchs. Seated upon the haiseki I see each one in turn and am too awed to meditate deeper for I know they will actually appear and I will speak to them in this public place; they are walking about; one is scratching his foot; one turns round, although he is talking to someone else, and says, "Ah, yes" as I recite his name. I realise that they are dressed as monks and that the rest of the people here wear highly-coloured clothing, including, I suspect, myself. I am a monk; and here I am going around in all the colours of the rainbow. Yesterday I asked, "What is next?" and was told, "You will know when the time comes." *My* purpose is to be a monk—that I *know*. I now realise how to be one; I must not wander around up here when there is nothing else to do and there is not a ceremony on; if there is no ceremony I must *make* one. Thus I *make* the monk appear. This morning here I am calling to the Patriarchs saying, "Hey, monk, how do I become a monk?" I find myself grinning suddenly upon the haiseki as I am watching the whole line go by. This *is* the right thing; I come to Morning Service; whether anybody else comes is not my problem. I can walk around on the shore and enjoy the Buddha Land if I wish to or I can take the next step.

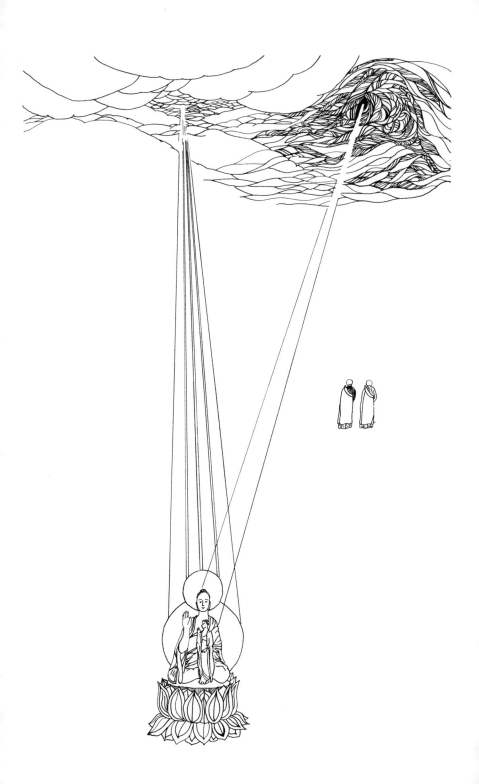

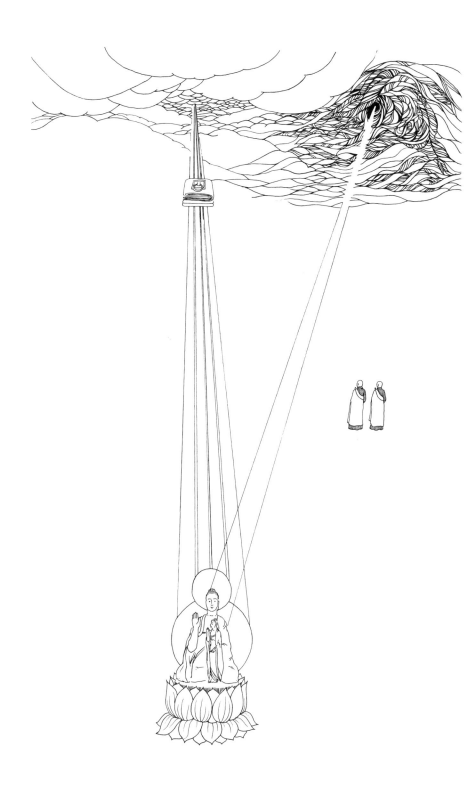

PLATES XXV AND XXVI:— ORDINATION
AND GRADUATION.

A monk is studying my notes this morning. He suddenly knows that the golden figure in the sky, with the white-clad figure of Shakyamuni standing with it, is an emanation of the Cosmic Buddha; this is why it appears as old gold in colour rather than bright gold. Even heavenly beings cannot behold the brightness of the Lord of the House so that which is seen in the Buddha Land is His emanation. The monk is told that the Buddhas do not wish the lotuses to come too close; the beings therein must drink in the Cosmic Buddha through his emanation, as the lotus blossoms of this world drink in the sun's rays, and take their knowledge and certainty of Him back down their stems to this world for the good of all beings.

It is evening and I am again meditating. I am no longer in my lotus blossom in the sea but moving through the air above it and there is a golden being dressed as a monk accompanying me. We are moving through the air without wings or clouds to help us; just going upward and upward at an incredible pace, moving as if from left to right at a gradual angle for a very great distance. I look down at the heavenly place far below and see the little building housing the fountain on top of the hill with its rivulets streaming down to the sea. It is very pleasant but this does not matter. We are going up, I know not where; I knew this morning that staying in a heavenly place was not for me.

We come to a place where there are golden beings and descend a little to greet them for a moment or two. We then continue straight upward and then slant to the left instead of the right and, after a certain distance, come down a little again to greet some more golden beings whom I know to be the past Buddhas. We continue up and up, again angling to the right.

Since I have been in this place I have been wearing bright colours like the other beings here. As I travel with this golden being I can, as it were, see myself; and now the bright colours fall away together with my form; I see it and them constantly falling forward and dropping away from me as the skins may be peeled from an onion. I ask, "Should I go higher?" and I am told, "You should go back; you are needed." I return at once as the Lord requests and do that which it is my duty to do. I am told that the journey will continue as soon as I lie down. It is bed-time; I am absolutely exhausted; I can eat nothing.

It is four o'clock in the morning. I know that the journey is about to continue but I do not wish to awaken Daizui although I know he has to be here. He comes in when I call him and the journey continues.

From where I am now I can see the back of the emanation of the Cosmic Buddha. I and the golden monk are standing to the right of four yellow-golden rays. I look up and perceive that three of these rays come forth from a bright place within golden-edged clouds; the fourth ray comes forth from a tiny white spot in a patch of absolutely black sky. The four rays touch the back of the emanation. I know that I *must* close my eyes; I feel something compelling them to close. Daizui has his back to me; somehow we both know that this must not be seen with mortal eyes. I do not know what to do and Daizui asks the Lord if he may see what I should do without looking at me and is told he may. I ask what to do and am told, "Be content. Do not seek to go higher." Wholeheartedly I answer, "I *am* content." As I say this my entire body is thrilled through and through with liquid light. It enters through every pore, through fingers, toes, head, sides, through every orifice of my body. Five times the light thrills through me; I ask before each one, "What more may I do?" Finally it gathers and pierces me in the hara but I feel no pain. I ask, "How may I show my gratitude to the Buddhas and Patriarchs?" and am told with a smile, "You always wanted to be a *real* monk." Great clouds of yellow-gold pass in waves over my closed eyes.

I ask Daizui what is happening and he says he sees a kind of ordination. There is an exquisite, golden Kesa in the sky; when the time comes for me to open my eyes the highly-coloured clothes I have been wearing will no longer be there; instead there will be the form of a monk. He says it will soon be time for me to go back down; this is the last such journey I shall take for a while. I ask what I should do and am told to go back to the sea; my work is to be a gardener who helps the lotus blossoms to grow straight.

I go at once to Shasta's meditation hall. Just before the kaishaku sound for the end of meditation I find myself again in the Buddha Land. I am standing both on the haiseki of Shasta's Hondō and on that of the Dai Kaidō of the Buddha Land. The Sangha stretches to infinity in both directions on either side of me in ranks of five. The first four rows on each side are golden both of body and robes; then come those wearing coloured robes and those in black stretching back and back, lost in the shadows of the great hall.

The altar is the same emanation of the Cosmic Buddha that I have seen in the sky and Shakyamuni, clad in white, stands with him as before. He comes and goes from the emanation to me many times during the ceremony as if teaching me what to do. I am very afraid to look up but all are gentle and accept me com-

pletely; I do not need to fear rejection. Now I *know*
that when we say "Homage to the Buddha" it is the
Cosmic Buddha of which we speak; "Homage to the
Dharma" is homage given to Shakyamuni Buddha who
gives us the Teaching in this world; "Homage to the
Sangha" is homage given to all beings who train themselves to reach the waveless sea and then go on beyond
to the True Monastery of the Lord of the House. There
is but one Sangha, pure and undivided. Men and
women, no matter of what school of Buddhism, meet
there as equals before the Lord and are greeted by the
Great Monks with respect. As I recite the Patriarchal
Line I only catch a fleeting glimpse of the Seven Buddhas but, from Makakashyo on, the golden monks
answer to their names—Makakashyo, Ananda, Shôna-
washyu[1]—they are all here—the first five on my left,
the next five on my right, then back again to the left—
each recognises me in turn. Some wonder why I stop to
bow at their names; they are but monks as I. From
here on I must make no bows when I recite their names;
what I was taught concerning such things in Sôji-ji does
not apply; now I must learn what the Lord wishes to
be done and not concern myself with worldly sectarian-
ism. The Hôkyozammai speaks Truth:— 'Separated do
the sects become by setting up of doctrines, practices,
and these become the standards that we know of all
religious conduct. Even should we penetrate these doctrines, practices, and then delusive consciousness flows
through the eternal Truth, no progress shall we make.'
From now on I will sit up straight in the presence of
the Buddhas and Patriarchs as is their will. I go outside
the temple. The beings in their highly-coloured clothes
stroll along the shore. I still have not seen the colour of
my robes.

---

1. The three Patriarchs after Shakyamuni Buddha.

I return to my house at Shasta; I am intensely cold. I ask Daizui to ask what this ceremony was and learn that it was my graduation. I now know that one is ordained many times. Long ago I was ordained by the Sangha that we see in this world and I was re-ordained when I was ill in Oakland and re-Transmitted also; both after leaving the iron pillar behind. Now I have been ordained again in the Monastery of the Lord of the House—when, and if, it shall please Him I will go for my Transmission in this exquisite place.

It is the same day. I am in a boat with Shakyamuni Buddha upon the sea. He is inspecting buds again and very anxious that, as a new gardener, I understand the importance of strong stems without which the plants will die; he is much more interested in stems than he is flowers. I am wearing black robes; what joy to be a new monk in the temple of the Lord and to work in His garden. 'The true monk regards the world as a playground or a beautiful garden' says the Transmission Book; there are no truer words.

It is morning. In my eagerness to do my job yesterday I made several mistakes which resulted in several of these precious monks being harmed. I am devastated with horror; how could I have been so stupid; it takes time to grow stems; it does not happen overnight. Because of my stupidity I almost ruined one. As I meditate upon this, grieving, the white figure descends and walks with me beside the sea; He puts an arm around me and comforts me. I must remember to ask Him each time before I do something; I must remember that I am only the gardener and not think that I need no help.

PLATE XXVII:– THE FIVE ASPECTS
OF THE MONK.

It is the morning of the 8th. of November. There
are five golden columns of light coming out of my
body. They move up and are now coming out of the
lotus blossom upon my head, arranged towards the
back of it. I see the mark upon my forehead very clearly as a Buddha image; the five light columns are arranged
on either side of it with one in the centre at the back. I
ask Daizui to come in quickly for I know that I need
him. It is absolutely imperative that I am not alone; it
is as if I need my Chief Junior with me. I have to be so
still at these times; even to ask a question of the Lord
of the House seems to be too much of a disruption. I
have to be so still and so continuously open; willing to
do whatsoever is required or needed; to break this
silence even by so much as to talk to the Lord is too
much. Daizui asks what I should do and is told, "Go in
and out." "Where do I go?" "Go up one of the five
columns of light." He knows there are five although he
has seen and heard nothing. "I do not know how to go
up. How do I do it?" "Just go up." "I am willing." I go
up the first column of light and realise that it is the one
that comes from the black clouds in the sky that I saw
before my ordination. Although I am going towards
the tiny spot in the blackness it always remains light.
The emanation of the Cosmic Buddha comes over from
the bright columns to enter the one that I am in just
above me and I understand that this is how earth penetrates heaven. No matter how great the darkness there
is still light to be found therein by those who truly
look. In the darkest place, even on the side of the black

lotus, is to be found the true teaching that saved me from despair—NOTHING MATTERS. One can jump into hell so long as one is looking up. At all times the Buddha is appearing in hell and in this world. 'Within all light is darkness but explained it cannot be by darkness that one-sided is alone. In darkness there is light but, here again, by light one-sided it is not explained,'— the Sandōkai speaks Truth.

I return; this then is the meaning of going in and out. Do I go up the second column?" "Yes." "How do I do it? I am willing." I am infused with ecstasy in every part of my being. It is so beautiful; I am being taken possession of, infused with a luminescent, spiritual 'water.' I do not know what to do next—I never seem to know what to do—I am told to go up the third column but nothing happens. "I am willing to go; to be absolutely possessed; what do I do?" I go up the third column of light; this is where I was ordained; I feel I should go no further. "How far should I go?" "Only go halfway to meet it." Out of the golden-edged clouds above comes the white figure of Shakyamuni; it enters my body; it keeps coming, hundreds upon hundreds of it, faster and faster, entering through the Buddha mark upon my forehead and coming to rest in my hara. It begins to slow down. This is heaven penetrating earth; the Dharma constantly given to those willing to receive it—it is the same as the light flashing off the pillar in that dark place; the Lord is to be found in all places if we do but believe. The black lotus and the flashing light are entrances both to life and death.

I am back again. "There are two left. Do I go up any more?" "Yes, go up the next one." "I am willing." I am again infused but this time it is different; it is a golden infusion that is also a bath; I am being bathed in this golden infusion of spiritual 'water' as in a fountain. I am thrilled through and through again and again; it is cold, a very strange cold. Daizui touches me; it is as if I am cold from the inside out. The words go through my mind that this is a spiritual marriage but the word 'marriage' is not quite right. It is the meaning of the fact that there is always holy water to be found in the master's head. This bath is so exquisite.

There is one column left. "Should I go up?" "You may." The tone of the answer is different. "Well, *should* I?" "If you wish." "Is it wrong?" "No." "Would it be dangerous?" "It is all right," and there is a little smile as if to say that it is good that I ask all these questions instead of just going up. I say, "All right, I will go up," and am infused again and then I am back. I see the Buddha mark as I enter; I am incredibly cold. I ask what these five columns are and am told they are the aspects of the monk and the sunbeams of the teaching; the first is the Buddha's appearance in this world, and in all others, if only we will look with unclouded eyes—thus we can hear true teaching even in the darkest place—the golden Buddha descends through the tiny hole to hell—if *only* we will look up!—the second is eternal love which we can feel even in the pangs of hell if we truly understand the Buddha's teaching; the third the teaching which is always entering us if only we are willing for it to do so; the fourth is the fountain of the Lord's wisdom and the fifth I do not yet understand. These five columns bend over and shed millions of seeds; I watch them fall. In all these meditations I am told, "Be very careful; be *very* careful." Thus I make no move before asking what to do; I must be *very* still. I may not close my eyes; I am told "NO" when I do; it does not want me to completely leave this world; it is imperative I have an anchor here. I ask if the bath will get warm and almost get a chuckle; yet it does not feel as cold water feels; it is an exquisite sensation. The words, "The diamond sceptre's branches five" go through my mind. The seeds are the seeds of the teaching; thus is Daizui told.

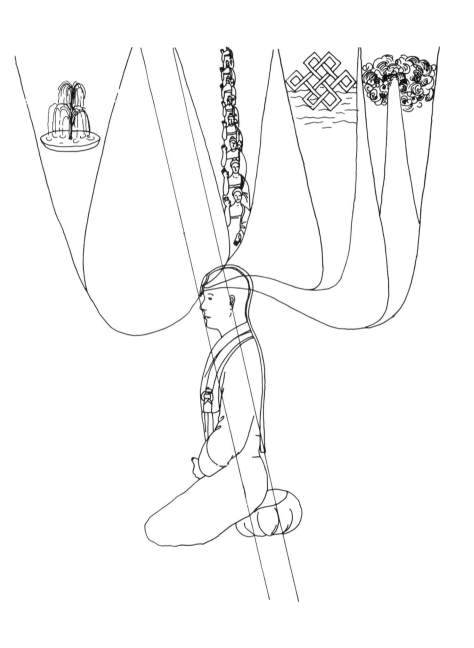

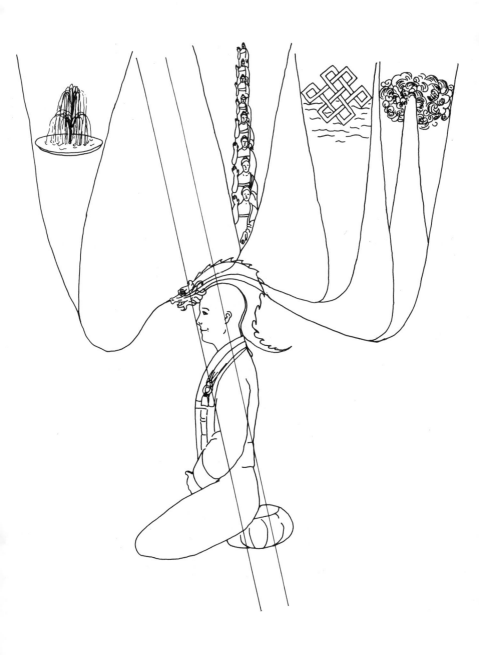

PLATES XXVIII, XXIX AND XXX:—
RECEIVING THE TEACHING.

It is the morning of the 9th. of November; I awaken with the five columns of light very clear; they come out of the head of a clear, crystal-like nyoi.[1] The first column has already been explained; around its end is the darkness and the column itself comes from the white spot with the seated Buddha a little distance down from it—and yet it encloses the darkness—thus does earth penetrate heaven and is enfolded within it. There is a cloud at the end of the second column in which there is an intricate, square knot—the love-knot of eternity. At the top of the third column is Shakya-muni as the Dharma constantly descending—thus heaven penetrates earth. At the top of the fourth column is the fountain of the Lord's wisdom the water of which, when one is bathed therein, is infused through every fibre of one's body—thus there is always holy water in the master's head. The fifth I still do not know. And now I know what the nyoi is—it is exactly the shape of my spine—it is indeed my spine. The nyoi head bends over my head and its front rests on my brow; the Buddha mark is in its centre and from it radiate the five columns of light; two on each side and one from the top. It is now a great lotus pod and my spine is its stalk and the columns of light cause the seeds to be shed. It changes again and now has the shape of a dragon—my spine is its spine, its head is over my head. It has five great whiskers that become the columns of light. The

---

1. That which a priest carries during ceremonies symbolising the fact that he is celebrant.

117

dragon is the symbol of the defender of the Truth—I understand that thus must I become; not only must the nyoi be used to show the defence of the Truth—one must *be* the nyoi that *defends* the Truth as also one must *be* the lotus blossom that *sheds* the seeds of the Truth. Sometimes I will be a dragon and again sometimes a lotus. The nyoi changes again and now its head is that of an elephant with five trunks each of which becomes one of the columns of light. The elephant is the symbol of holiness—thus I must use the nyoi of my body to express the Truth through holiness of life. The fountain in the fourth column sends forth golden water wherein are bathed the hearts, bodies and minds of beings. 'The absolute upright' is the stem of the lotus, the spine of my physical body; how important it is to sit correctly when meditating. Now, too, I understand the meaning of 'the diamond sceptre's branches five' for I am indeed the diamond sceptre.

Within each one of us lies the Treasure House; all we have to do is unlock the door for ourselves. When I stand upon the haiseki, that which stands there *is* the living nyoi; I hold only the symbol of that which I am; sometimes I stand there as a lotus blossom shedding the teaching, sometimes I am the defender of the Truth and sometimes I must *be* the personification of holiness and again as hard and radiant as a diamond—and I must be all of these at all times and each of them at all times. This is the meaning of being a priest. And when I show each of these aspects I must also show how, in that aspect, earth penetrates heaven, eternal love is demonstrated, heaven penetrates earth, all is bathed in the fountain of the Lord's wisdom—as yet I do not understand the fifth. There are five aspects of each of these five columns of light but I do not know their meaning yet. The fountain in the fourth clearly indicates *anicca*, change, but that is all I know so far.

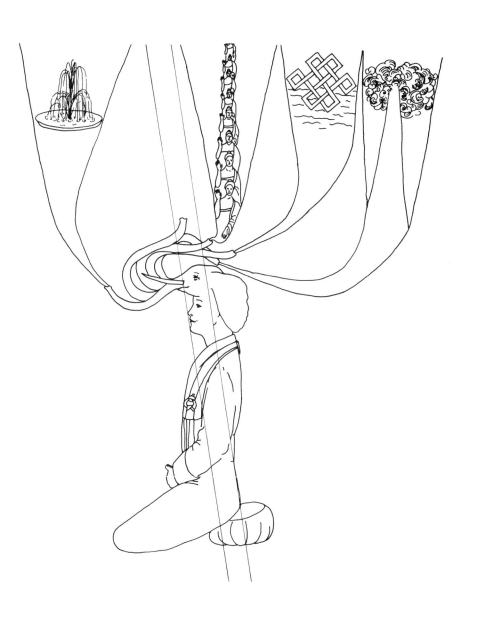

The explanation of the gasshō is here also. The five fingers of the right hand signify the worlds of humans, titan asuras, animals, hungry ghosts and hells whilst those of the left hand signify the Buddha, Bodhisattvas, one's own enlightenment, enlightenment by others and heaven. When I passed through the dark place all things were passed on the right; now all things are seen on the left. When the two hands are correctly joined earth penetrates heaven and heaven penetrates earth. When heaven and hell become one the Buddha Land is indeed here and now.

My head wishes to make one long, perpetual bow; the five columns of light stream upward. 'The state of mind must always be respectful and modest'—so states the explanation of the gasshō. Man, in his little knowledge, believes he knows what pleasure is but worldly pleasures leave behind them an emptiness and flatness; he who experiences that which I am experiencing knows a fullness that is beyond human comprehension. Now indeed I *know* what is my work in the monastery of the Lord. It is so important that the stem of every lotus be perfect; it is imperative that I do not allow these precious monks who live in Shasta to make any mistakes whatsoever in their training. If the stem is perfect the blossom will be magnificent. Then, and only then, will they become living nyois of the Lord.

PLATE XXXI:— THE IRON MAN.

It is just before breakfast of the same day. In my hara there are two golden doors standing wide open and, inside them, is a golden lotus. I am conscious that the lotus on my head has changed from pink and indigo to gold, the five columns of light come out from it and the mark of the Buddha is in the centre of it and then again in the centre of my forehead. Light is coming out of the flower. This is the meaning of the doors of the temple always standing open wide, the doors of the heart, never being closed to anyone who asks for help. Everyone has entrance to the kaidō, the shadowy hall within themselves; all they have to do is knock. All they have to do is ask and they will be answered. The light streams out of the flower—it is the light with which I was infused last night—the infusing with gold—it comes out of the flower and colours my flesh until my entire body is golden. Then comes Maka-kashyo; this time I am with him as a golden being and the two of us travel up and to the right. Suddenly we start going straight up; I am being infused with golden spiritual 'water' again. We are absorbed right into the fifth golden column of light and there is neither of us left; just two beings that are, and were, and will be part of, and not apart from, the golden column going upwards and upwards; there is nothing else. I ask what to do and am told to go on. I choose to come back in order to be able to bring this back to you. I ask, "Am I wrong to return?" and am told, "Your choice. It does not matter." "Have I made a choice between dying and living?" "No."

Now the golden light that comes out of the clouds and the fifth column of light turn into the iron pillar that I saw in the dark place, the Iron Man. This pillar penetrates the universe from one end to the other, piercing me through my forehead, entering the earth at the base of my spine. I can go back up this pillar at any time I wish or come down in the same way; it is that which makes heaven and earth one. I am bathing again in the golden light, there is ecstasy in the infusing of my body.

I took the Bodhisattva vow long ago; I keep it still. 'However innumerable beings are I vow to save them'—thus I choose to come back—but even after the vow, to do so is *still* a voluntary act; the Lord does not insist upon the keeping of the vow.

This iron pillar, which is the entrance to heaven and hell, is the direct route by which we go, in the twinkling of an eye, to the Lord during the first, or Penetration of Heaven, kenshō. When we learn to harmonise heaven and earth we are permitted to go slowly that the way may be made plain for us to show to all living things. He who would fulfill the Bodhisattva vow *must* reach this stage.

GYOKUKO

PLATE XXXII:– THE TRUE BEING.

I stay all day in a state of suspended animation. It is now evening and Daizui, although he did not see what I did, is in the same state as I as a result of asking questions for me. I was very frightened after I chose not to continue to go up this morning for I started to come back down and was going into darkness; I did not wish to go into darkness. I started coming back up again and have remained suspended between darkness and light during the entire day.

I am needed to do some work but both Daizui and I feel very strange; he needs to come back. I tell him to come back and this releases him. I know that I too must somehow come back into myself and stop standing in the column of light. I ask if this is the right thing to do and am told "Yes" through Daizui. I find myself coming back down the fifth column of light and enter by the Buddha mark on my forehead. I come to rest in the centre of the flower within my hara. I must *not* forget the words, "Go in and out." I am beginning to run a bad cold and, not feeling well, I do not wish to take any more spiritual 'journeys' for a little. But it is obvious that I am going to continue. During the night I am conscious of sitting still in the centre of the golden lotus. The doors are open to the world and golden light streams out of them. That which is standing in the centre of the golden flower is now the new-born Buddha with one hand pointing up and the other down; He is standing in the centre of the column of light which has entered my head and this column is in the centre of the golden flower. The column and the

Baby Buddha melt into a diamond nyoi which is exactly the shape of my spine; it changes into a lotus blossom, then into a lotus pod, then into a bud, into a dragon with five whiskers which curl up and become the five columns of ascending light and into the elephant with five trunks that curl up into these same five columns. It constantly changes from one to the other. I understand that sometimes I am the diamond sceptre which penetrates the universe; sometimes I am the lotus blossom, sometimes I pour out the seeds of the Dharma, sometimes I am a new blossom and at other times a new bud; sometimes I am the defender of the faith and sometimes I am holy. And all of these things find their root in the centre of the golden lotus within my hara. I am very frightened that I cannot bend because of the rigidity of the diamond sceptre; the diamond sceptre just then becomes my spine and I am even more frightened that I cannot bend; and the Baby Buddha still stands within the golden lotus. As I move the diamond sceptre becomes the lotus and I am able to bend; the stem is always flexible!

I stay thus until the morning. The five columns come out sometimes from the Buddha mark on my forehead and sometimes from the five points of the golden crown, or lotus, upon my head; at other times they form the column at the base of which is the Baby Buddha. I now know the meaning of all five. They truly are the aspects of the monk; the first is earth penetrating heaven; the second, the knot of eternity; the third, heaven penetrating earth; the fourth, the putting on of the golden kesa which is within the fountain of the Buddha's Wisdom, the bathing within its radiance; the fifth, "the ability to die whilst sitting and standing which transcends both peasant and sage"—the right to go to heaven or hell if the intention is right—to help all living things. My wish for now is just to be a monk that I may take all beings with me to this exquisite place.

PLATE XXXIII:– THE REAL MONK.

It is morning. The golden doors of my hara stand wide open; the Baby Buddha stands within the golden flower. Light streams upward from him to the gold-rimmed clouds and streams from them back downwards to him. Another ray comes from the clouds and enters the Buddha mark upon my forehead. From this mark also emanates the five columns which are the five aspects of the monk; sometimes they are separate and sometimes they form the one column within me. The lotus blossom is upon my head; sometimes it is a golden crown.

Today is the first day of my life that I have ever *wanted* to wear a golden rakhsu, or ever felt that I had the right to do so. Now I must not wear anything else. When you receive the kesa of gold brocade it should be worn with honour and with pride.

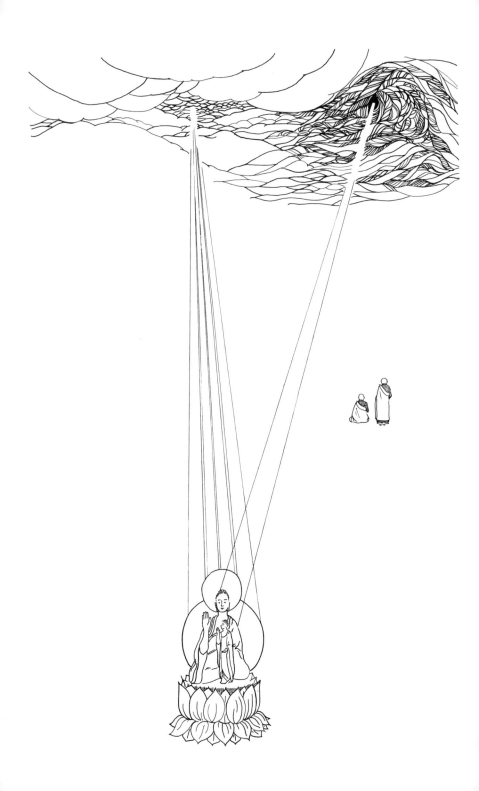

PLATE XXXIV:– THE FIRST COLUMN–
ETERNAL MEDITATION.

It is morning. I am again going upwards above the Buddha Land. I ascend to the place where I was ordained together with Makakashyo. I ask what I should do and am told to wait. I see both Makakashyo and I quite clearly; we are both golden. We wait for a long time; I am told I should not be standing and I sit down. After a long time I am told, "I shall not call you today. You should go back down soon." I immediately return.

When I meditate I must do so in the place of or-dination–the mind of a beginner is the purest of all minds–'end and beginning here return unto the source.' When the Lord calls I will go to him; whilst waiting for his call I will do his will; this is eternal meditation. This Shasta *is* the Buddha Land; these trainee monks are *in* the monastery of the Lord. How great *is* the Lord; how joyous his service. Our petty minds argue about their own concepts of Him and quarrel about sectarian emanations–thus he is divided into a Christian God, a Cosmic Buddha, Allah and what not besides. But That which Is, the Lord of the House, whilst laughing at our cardboard replicas, sends down His rays to all so that, if they truly look, they may see beyond their own facades. This is true love in all its glory. *Homage* to the Buddha, *Homage* to the Dharma, *Homage* to the Sangha.

Eternal meditation is the meaning of this first column of light and its second aspect, its first being its appearance which I described before. Even in the dark-est place the Truth may be seen and heard; thus medi-tation *is* possible for eternity; there is always light in darkness and the Buddha may be seen therein if we have the willingness to look. The third aspect of eternal meditation is its use; its use is to bring peace and freedom in all the situations that life brings. Sitting in this eternal meditation I watch that which the world regards as good or bad come and go as reflections in a mirror; all is ever changing; the mirror is clear, it does not retain the reflections.

The purpose of eternal meditation is the *Cessation of Suffering*, the third of the Buddha's Four Noble Truths for, by holding on to nothing and pushing nothing away, I am free of attachments. The fifth aspect of this first column of light is its root, its oneness with all the other aspects, the oneness that penetrates the universe.

Every time I meditate I ascend the first column of light; earth penetrates heaven whenever Zazen is truly done; this is the full meaning of the first of the five branches of the diamond sceptre.

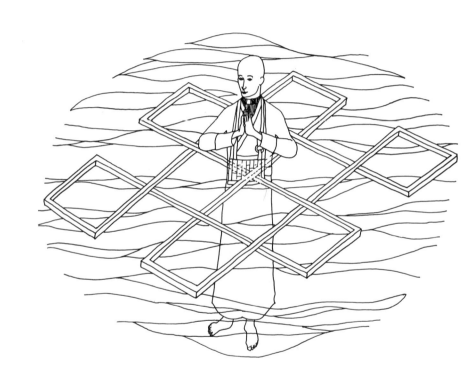

PLATE XXXV:– THE SECOND COLUMN–
THE CLEANSING WATER OF THE SPIRIT.

"Go in and out," I was told when I saw the five branches of the diamond sceptre. I did not fully understand the importance of this at the time. There have been those, in these last few weeks, who have been horrified by what I have told them; there have been those who have sworn that I am ruining the teaching, those who have gone away; how sad I am for them. For days and days I grieved until my sickness came back; and then I went again into meditation, even deeper than ever before, and now I *know* the use of these five branches and I know so much more besides. Grieving over the loss of these, I ask the Lord deeply what is the mistake I have made, what harm I have done–please show me if I have done harm for indeed I intend none. And we were told, Daizui and I, that the answer was to be found in the five branches of the diamond sceptre, the five columns of light, and I knew that it was within the second column. For the Lord indeed does take care of all his beings; it is not for me to usurp the place of the Lord. That they go or come is not my problem; that they stay is not my problem. If they turn away from me the Lord still does not turn away from them. If I feel anguish at their loss it is because there is in me still some clinging and herein lies the use of the second column–the washing in eternal love. I offer up both them and me into this column; I watch them washed within this luminescent water of the spirit. The Lord neither rejects anything nor holds on to it; he washes, he cleanses, he loves and he waits. Thus should we do also with all fear–offer it up to the Lord in the second column, watch it washed and cleaned. This is also true of all past lives, all the impregnations, the vasana. We need nothing more to cleanse us from the vasana than our own willingness to offer it to the Lord and to love it, and not reject it, as He does, as we pass it on; His love indeed will cleanse all things; there is no need for any assistance from another being such as I. Indeed the way in which the ancient Buddhas did this was the right way—all is achieved through the turning of the Wheel of the Law; all is achieved through the way in which a man follows his breath when he meditates.

I have been given a great and wonderful opportunity—an opportunity which is open to all—to know how this is done, to know how to live free from fear, from grief, from pain; to *know the cessation of suffering* for this is the *purpose* of all five light columns; all things may be offered to the Lord in this second column and washed clean in His love—the seeming uncleanness caught in the Knot of Eternity which is Eternal Love.

Each of these branches, each of these columns of light, I have said has five aspects. Herein is the third aspect of the second column. The first was its appearance and the second its meaning which I described earlier. The third aspect, its use, is the washing of all doubt and fear and grief and sorrow, and the cleansing of the pain of others. Herein lies the meaning of the Ekō, "The great saint turns the Wheel of the Law and thereby shows many aspects of the Truth."[1] By offering those that attack me, physically or spiritually, to the Lord they are cleansed gently in His love and passed on; thus the Lord converts all things to His own good use. All four aspects of each branch dissolve into the fifth, the root, as do all branches of the diamond sceptre,—all dissolve into one, the fifth,—the one great

1. See *Zen is Eternal Life*, p. 306.

column which joins earth and heaven, the column that penetrates the universe. For indeed there is no difference between earth and heaven; this Shasta and the Buddha Land are one—they penetrate each other mutually. If a man would be truly free he must not hold on to his petty ideas nor to his opinions; all should be offered up this second column to be washed by the Lord that he may be bathed later in the spirit on the return journey of the turning of the Wheel. 'The Lord neither discards everything unholy nor does not discard it;' this is the use of the Knot of Eternity; within it there is nothing clean or unclean.

There is so much to learn; I must study much more deeply and in much more detail. 'However innumerable Dharmas are I vow to master them'—I will keep the Bodhisattva vow. I sit in peaceful meditation; the attackers come—I offer them up the second column to the Lord who cleanses them gently and passes them on. Mara, too, should be dealt with in this way. This is one meaning of 'offering merit;'—how unfortunate is that translation! It no longer matters that people believe, or do not believe, what I have written for I know it to be the Truth; there is just sitting still, sitting still, sitting still—for eternity.

PLATE XXXVI:– THE THIRD COLUMN–
HEAVEN PENETRATES EARTH.

It is the morning of the 22nd. of December. I am sitting in the centre of the third column of light looking down. At the bottom of the first column I see one of those who have gone away; he is looking up the first column through the tiny hole in the dark clouds which are now below me. He comes up the second light column of his own free-will to wash in the water of the Lord; the others wash there also.

I already know the appearance and the meaning of this third column; this is its use. I must stay in meditation with my heart always open to those who have gone away; only then will they feel free to decide to come or go. I want them to come so very much but I must not chase after them; if I do I enter into duality and again sunder body and mind by leaving my true place–this can only result in more suffering. To leave the meditative state is to turn the Wheel of the Law in the wrong direction; it is to turn it into the Wheel of Karma.

This third column is like the first; they are both eternal meditation, as is the fifth, but the first is meditation from earth to heaven and the third meditation from heaven to earth: the fifth melds the two into one. I cannot help these disciples by joining their darkly clouded delusions; I can help them by staying in meditation so that they may have the opportunity to see the light for themselves. I must stay in this state at all times when dealing with worldly matters of whatever nature–government officials, lawyers, people caught up in fame and gain–all must be met from the standpoint of meditation with the mind at peace and the heart open—only thus can heaven penetrate earth and the harmony of body and mind be preserved. Without trying to gain a victory, knowing that there is no victory to be won or lost, I meet the so-called worldly *as they are* and *know* that they are Buddhas.

There has been much disharmony caused by my experiencing this kenshō during the past month; one of those who have left has done so because of it. I have shown the jewel and people ask its worth: and yet I must show it at all times. Here is another use of the third column of light; I must live in the world and in the sky with no glimpse of my inner life to be caught. I must walk about in the world but remain still looking at it from the centre of the third column; I must view it as if looking downwards from the sky.

It is the thirty-first of December. This morning I see some impregnations of a former life. I am a tartar in the tenth century who combats his boredom by taking part in jousts that require him to ride leaning sideways out of the saddle so as to be able to slash at the legs of the horse ridden by his opponent with a curved sword. At the time of his death he overbalances and is trampled by an on-coming horse in the chest-area. The joust is held in a boggy area and his heavy chain-mail causes him to sink. There are people nearby but, for some reason, they do not help him. His best friend leads up his horse, a chestnut, and stands still looking down at him; this karmic stream is now one of the disciples who has gone away—I see his fur jacket and hat, as well as his features clearly. All that is left to view of the tartar is his chain-mail helmet and his black, handle-bar moustache surmounted by his nose and brilliant blue eyes. He makes no sound although he knows he is dying and his friend is doing nothing to help him. He sees the right, top quarter of a mongolian monk in a maroon robe out of his left eye, his right is now buried in the bog, and resolves next rebirth to *be* a monk; nothing he has found in this life has combatted boredom; all he has achieved is the killing of many horses and some men—all to no purpose. He becomes a monk in his next life and, through learning to meditate, cleans the impregnations that his cruel acts have left upon that monk's skhandas; he was a good monk and so I have no debts to pay for his or the tartar's deeds. But I can learn several lessons from his actions and it is for this purpose that the Lord of the House has permitted me to see this past life. "Tartar friend, if you had known of the five columns of light, if you had known how to turn the Wheel of the Law, you would not die thus in confusion, musing on the faithlessness of friends and the uselessness of your life. I do not need to convert you; you were converted long ago by a faithful monk but I will gladly do a memorial ceremony for you out of gratitude for the teaching your life gives me; I will study it in detail."

If this tartar had meditated he could have ascended the third column and enjoyed the world with a peaceful heart, he would have known from whence help came in time of affliction. He would have needed no external excitement to combat his boredom for he would forever have been fulfilled from within and, through the use of the fifth column, he could have united heaven and earth for all to see. He was a great jouster but all he had to show as his life's work was skill in killing horses and the aches, pains, bruises and deaths of his fellow contestants. Small wonder he died vowing to be a monk when the Lord asked the inevitable question, "What is your purpose for living?" How could he say to the Lord, "My purpose is to knock others off horses by killing the horses?" The greatest prayer I know is, "Lord, give me the time and the knowledge to make the *right* decisions concerning my life *before* I meet You face to face."

But this tartar's kōan was the same as that of the white tiger and of Alexia, the woman of whom I spoke earlier. All three wanted freedom to be truly themselves—and of the three only the tiger knew who and what he was at the time of his capture—a tiger; how sad that man confused his mind at the time of death. The tartar tried to escape from what he considered to be the "mundaneness" of being an ordinary man by doing daring acts—he had no knowledge of the fact that true freedom is to be found within. The tiger, although he knew in the beginning what he was and was happy to be what he was, thought that freedom was only possible if he were not in a cage as a result of taking notice of man's delusions. Down the centuries there have been many, many monks who once inherited the stream of karma that has now come down to me. All tried to penetrate the Truth; some by meditation, others by prayer. All were true seekers of the Way, whether Christian or Buddhist; many were content with heaven and some with the lake of quietism. These were good people but, fearing the loss of the little freedom they had gained, they went into hardness and coldness and lovelessness through ascetic practices—and in so doing lost their little freedom! One of them, the organist of a Christian monastery, tried to find freedom by burying himself completely in his music but freedom was not to be found therein. One is tempted to say that this is a step up from killing horses and flogging oneself but music and learning are just as much impediments to finding true freedom as are horse-killing and flogging—and considerably more subtle. With luck one gets sick of killing and flogging in time, as did my karmic stream,—however, music and learning can compound delusion hugely. And then came Alexia. She did not enter religion; she tried to find freedom externally by helping those who were having a revolt—to gain freedom! The monks had tried to storm heaven and had failed—she would *snatch* freedom, both for herself and others—no wonder her dying thoughts were, "What did I do wrong? I was helping people become *free*." She took the opposite road to asceticism and ended up in the same place as the ascetics—confused. And all they had to do was ask the Lord for help in the *right way*. 'Knock and it shall be opened, seek and ye shall find' say the Christian scriptures—and still people ask the opinions of others and read books instead of *themselves* asking the Lord of the House directly and being willing to give *all* in return for the opening of the Treasure House. This Pillar of the Universe, this Iron Man, is owned by every single one of us; we are all the Children of Buddha: all we have to do is meditate sincerely and without doubt then we can look up and see the Buddha at all times, even in the darkest place, and look down on the turbulence of the world from the third column thus seeing the turmoil through the eyes of the Lord. Safe and secure in this place true freedom is ours for eternity.

It is from this position in the third column that the Zen Master answers questions put to him during Jōdō and Shōsan; the disciple is in the first column and the master in the third. The question is washed clean of delusion in the second column so that the master may make his answer the waters of the fountain of the Dharma in the fourth column—'the rain of Dharma comes as nectar down;' and these things are not 1, 2, 3 and 4 steps in a chain but one straight line which is the fifth column directly joining earth and heaven in luminescent darkness and dark brightness. Thus do master and disciple turn the Wheel of the Law and thereby show many aspects of the Truth. Parents are placed in the same position as the master by their children; how sad it is that no parent I have ever met has been secure in this third column. Their children have asked their very *real* questions in vain and have ended up like their parents with disharmony of body and mind, their True Nature torn from its true home sometimes for the rest of their lives. How wondrous is this third column; may *I* dwell there for eternity if the Lord of the House so wills.

As with the other columns, the fourth aspect of this third column is its purpose, the Cessation of Suffering, which I have just described along with its use, and the fifth aspect is its oneness with the other four columns.

PLATE XXXVII: – THE FOURTH COLUMN–
BATHED IN THE FOUNTAIN OF THE LORD.

It is the same day. I am standing by the fountain carrying the disciple whom I saw earlier to-day. I place him gently in the water and stand back. Two others come separately to the fountain and enter the water. I watch as they bathe. The fountain does not distinguish between them.

The appearance and meaning of the fourth column I have already mentioned; the use is exquisite. It is the bathing of all in the fountain of the Lord's love. The house over the fountain becomes the house over the new-born Buddha and the water of the fountain the sweet tea that is poured over His statue at Hannamatsuri. There is nothing clean or unclean in the Mind of the Lord; all are Buddha as are these and I must see this at all times no matter what they do. The Lord bathes all in the fountain of His love and I must do the same for I have nothing that is not of the Lord. 'Do not say that which is not true. The Wheel of the Law rolls constantly and lacks for nothing yet needs something; the sweet dew covers the whole world and within it lies the Truth'–the Fourth Precept–it should be kept absolutely. I must not even wonder about their Buddhahood for that is a form of lying. The Wheel of the Law needs expression in daily life, only then can the fountain of the Lord cover the world with sweet dew making His love manifest.

I have been becoming ill again during these last few days as a result of worrying about these disciples and I thought that perhaps I should not go to morning service for fear of a stroke or heart attack but I went anyway. Standing at the altar the thought struck me again and then something said, "So what?" So what indeed! What better place to die than facing the Lord before His altar? And in a flash the illness left me and I was whole again with no trace of illness whatsoever. I must remember to pour the water of the Lord's love over myself as well as others and trust Him absolutely. What these have done must not be allowed to cause me to doubt the Lord of the House; I will trust Him absolutely.

This fourth column holds the spring of compassion, as well as the water of love, and the seeds of the lotus. Sometimes that which comes forth is compassion, sometimes love, sometimes understanding, always is it the water for the healing of the spirit, always the teaching of the Dharma—that which fertilizes the harmony of body and mind. Every act that does *not* come forth from the egocentric I causes the water in the fountain to course more freely down the mountainside and flow into the waveless sea where it feeds the lotus blossoms giving those whose roots are under attack from Mara the strength, courage and faith to withstand his onslaughts. The best way I can help these disciples is by causing the water in the fountain to flow freely, not only for them, but for myself and all beings.

I remember sitting by the four streams of water on the hillside when I was wandering in heaven, dabbling my hands in the water, paddling in the waveless sea. Without knowing why then it was I who caused those streams from the fountain to dry up by not AT ONCE becoming a monk right then and going straight on instead of waiting to become a monk the following morning. How dangerous it is to just wander in, and enjoy, heaven! Unless the fountain flows constantly beings are lost and wander in Sansara for a seeming eternity. How wrong it was of me to waste my time thus. Who knows, if I had not done this would these disciples now be suffering as they are? I do Sange for this act and go on, determined not to make the same mistake again. How beauteous is this fountain. It bathes me too now that I have washed myself in the waters of Sange and confessed my fault before the Lord of the House. These four streams of water *are* the Four Noble Truths which bring forth compassion, love and wisdom. *Never* must they cease to flow.

There is so much more I do not yet know about this fountain but I do know that the purpose of the fourth column, as with the first three, is the Cessation of Suffering and its root is the root of the universe, the fifth column.

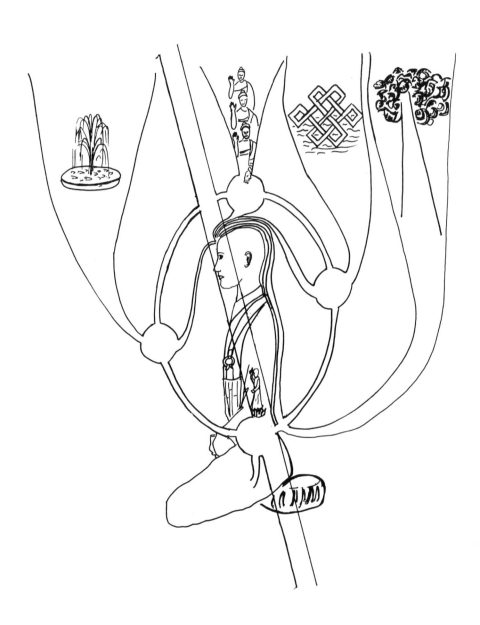

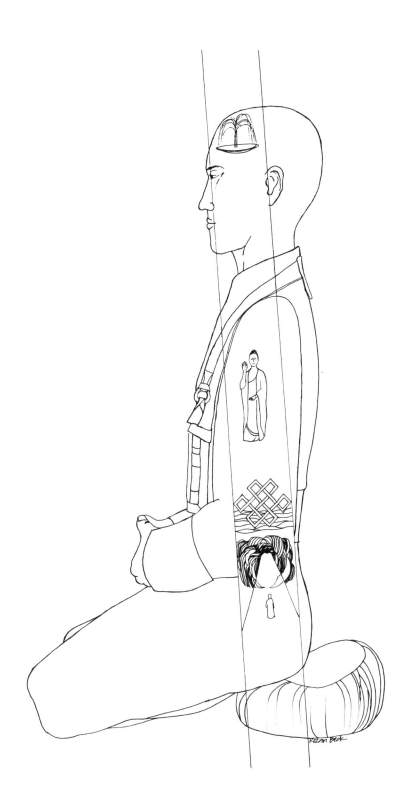

PLATE XXXVIII:– THE FIFTH COLUMN–
THE BUDDHA WITHIN.

    The new-born Buddha stands within the golden lotus within my hara in the centre of the column of light that is composed of the five light columns. His right hand points upward and his left down signifying the oneness of heaven and earth. The fifth column of light enters my forehead, passes through my body and out and down, thus it becomes the axis of the universe in which the Buddha sits. Sometimes, when all seems dark, I look up through the tiny hole in the first column to ask the help of the Lord, sometimes I wash myself clean of delusion in the second column, sometimes I am the emanation from the Cosmic Buddha in the third column so that others may be helped, sometimes I bathe, and am refreshed, in the fountain of the Lord's love and always I am still in my own place, the hara, the place where heaven and earth, body and mind, are one.

    This fifth column binds all together,–heaven, earth, body, mind, darkness, light–'Within all light is darkness but explained it cannot be by darkness that one-sided is alone. In darkness there is light, but here again by light one-sided it is not explained'–the Sandō-kai is a detailed explanation of the fifth column. This fifth column is the stem of the lotus, the physical body, the means by which man may know the Lord–"Your body is deeply significant," says Dōgen Zenji–it is by its means that I may know the Lord. My body suffers when I do not know the way to the Cessation of Suffering–it is the use of the body itself which *is* the way to the Cessation of Suffering. What an exquisite thing is this body—the root of the universe is exemplified therein.

When the five columns become the one the black clouds with the tiny hole are in the area of the bladder and kidneys, the misty cloud containing the knot of eternity is in the area of the intestines and stomach, the descending Shakyamuni in the area of the heart, lungs, liver and gall bladder, and the fountain in the head.

When I am in the blackness of despair my kidneys and bladder become sick and, if I remain in this state, may become diseased. When I am constantly grieving, worrying or doubting my stomach, spleen, pancreas and intestines become tense and, if I do not learn how to wash all of this grief, worry and doubt away by trusting the Lord completely and turning the Wheel of the Law, disease can result. When I become angry or frustrated I tense up the liver and gall bladder and cause the rending of the hara with its resulting disharmony of body and mind, constant rebirth, old age, disease and death. It is as if the two halves of the body become separate; the heart and lungs grow sad, for they long for the unity of the body, and a being becomes hard and resigned and, above all, terrified of death. Thus the lower half of the body, earth as it were, gains an unfortunate victory over the upper half, or heaven, binding a being to Sansara with seemingly no hope of freedom. When the brain tries to decide what to do the result is catastrophe and dis-ease of every description for every organ in the body is affected by the fear, despair, grief, worry, doubt, anger, frustration and sadness that result from its mistakes. *Only* the Lord of the House can *cause* the water of the fountain of wisdom, compassion and love to flow properly; the whole purpose of the brain is to furnish the Lord with accurate data—it is a computer in the service of the Lord; its job is *not* to usurp the Lord's position, just as man is in charge of mechanical computers at the present time and *they* must never be allowed to be in control of *him*.

The secret of this column is the willingness to look up rather than down. When in the black despair the tiny hole in the clouds is hard to see but it *is* there and, through it, we may *know* the Lord. *I* was in this place and would have died there if it had not been for my faith in my kenshō. *All* men can find the tiny hole of light, which is faith, if they will but look up. And then they must deal with their doubts and fears, their griefs, worries, anger and frustrations. Next they must wipe out the impregnations of their past lives. Then the dark pillar turns to light and the spirit ascends to meet its Lord, the brain cries out, "I give up; I am a servant and no master"—and it is a cry of relief! Majestically the Lord descends and sits in His rightful place; body and mind are one, heaven and earth are one, 'forsaking self the universe grows I.'[1] This book began as how a Zen Buddhist prepares for death and has become how a Zen Buddhist prepares for life.

For this fifth column comprises the Noble Eightfold Path;– Right Thought, Right Speech, Right Understanding, Right Action, Right Livelihood, Right Effort, Right Mindfulness, Right Meditation. In this way the Lord remains at peace in his own true place in eternal meditation; in this eternal meditation, eternal Zen, is to be found eternal life. The body dies physically when its purpose of existence is over—my purpose is to *be* a monk so now is not the time to die—one day the time will be right. A snail carries his house with him wherever he goes and he dies within his own house, that is within the Lord, the Root of the Universe, the Iron Man—perpetual darkness or perpetual light—or some-

---

1.*The Light of Asia*, Sir Edwin Arnold.

thing more—it is as we wish; it is not the problem of the Eternal Lord of the House.

The purpose of the fifth column, like the other four, is the Cessation of Suffering.

BIRTH

YOUTH

OLD AGE

right speech

right action

right livelihood

right effort

right thought

right understanding

Kozan

PLATE XXXIX:– THE PATH OF THE LOTUS.

The first step of the Noble Eightfold Path, which is the beginning of the Fourth Noble Truth, is Right Understanding and this I must show in simple faith, gratitude and humility. To *always* be open to believing everything that the Lord of the House tells to, or shows, me, to be absolutely grateful for *everything* that happens since it is a means of teaching, to feel neither fear nor elation, never to exhibit pride of achievement, to *know* that training is endless even if one has *reached* Buddhahood–*this* is Right Understanding. But this description began inadequately for Right Understanding transcends all dimensions, space; its joy cannot be described.

Unless there is *absolute* faith and obedience to the Lord's Will there can be *no* Right Understanding and, without Right Understanding, there can be no Right Thought, nor can there be any other steps of the Noble Eightfold Path. I developed this understanding because I was willing to go on believing, even in the darkest place at death's door, in the sight of the Truth that I had in 1963. Throughout all the years of seeming darkness, hatred, ill-will and grief that followed that kenshō I never doubted it. Thus, in those dark fourteen years was the seed of faith nourished, as is a seed in the dark earth, and that seed of faith grew and became the root, the axis mundi, Right Understanding, the Iron Man, the Fifth Column of Light which permeates the universe. How blessed are those seemingly dark years; I wrote of them in my diary hoping that, one day, someone going to Japan would be given pause; I wanted no one else to be hurt as was I. How wrong can a person be? Without the difficulties that I encountered in Japan and England this seed of faith would have been weak and, when put to the test in the darkest place, could not have borne fruit. When reading through my diary I know that I wanted to publish it for all the wrong reasons; now perhaps it *can* be published so that those who read it may know the measure of faith needed to help them in their own darkest hour and learn to bless, rather than curse, adversity; for it is on adversity that the seed of faith, once it has been TRULY PLANTED by the Penetration of Heaven kenshō, thrives; it is as rain to a plant—adversity gives strength in the darkest hour and causes the one who has had kenshō to show certainty of action.

This Right Understanding is the root of the lotus blossom—that from which the rest of the plant springs—that which enables the blossom to remain unwetted and unstained by the water that surrounds it whilst its roots remain in the mud; the roots of the lotus are nurtured in the mud just as Right Understanding can be nurtured in this world of delusion if only we use everything, including adversity, as an opportunity rather than an impediment to our training. Without those dark years there could have been no end to suffering, no finding of its cause and no certain knowledge of suffering's existence; there would, instead, have been the demi-life which is led by most people, a consciousness of dis-ease and a steady hardening of spirit and bitterness of mind as what seemed to be an inescapable inevitability was all that was known as life. I was not wrong to write the diary—only in wishing to publish it for the wrong reasons. If you would grow a lotus blossom you must plant the root of Right Understanding.

The second step of the Noble Eightfold Path is Right Thought and this is naturally the child of Right Understanding. When the understanding is *True* the thoughts become reality to the extent of taking shape and colour, thus confirming the Rightness of the Understanding; but I must not cling to that shape and colour any more than I must cling to emptiness. "Go in and out," we were told; "sometimes I raise the eyebrows of old Shakyamuni Buddha and sometimes I do not," said a great old master; these two sayings are the same; "we live in the world as if in the sky" is as this.

Right Thought is as the stem of the lotus, coming forth from the root of Right Understanding. Without that stem the plant is useless. Although hidden by the water I know it is there if a flower is visible; without it the flower will die. Just as there can be no stem without a root, so there can be no flower without a stem. Unseen both root and stem may be but, if there is a blossom, I *know* they are both there. If the blossom is always young and beautiful I know that the root and stem are healthy.

And what of the bud, Right Speech? Just as Right Thought comes out of Right Understanding, so is Right Speech the child of Right Thought. When the thought is wrong the speech becomes lying, coarse, irreverent, worrisome and incredible; when the stem becomes diseased because something has attacked the root, the lotus bud withers and dies. When faith is impaired, gratitude and joy die, thoughts become unreal, duality arises and there can be no trusting the speech of others let alone oneself.

Right Action is the result of Right Speech and Right Thought; it is the unfolding of the lotus flower. I may speak well but my actions must agree with that which I say otherwise I am as a bud that never blossoms. And if I do not blossom how can I cause others to wish to blossom? Right Livelihood for me is to *be* a monk; Right Livelihood for a lotus plant is to blossom— by so doing it causes men to gasp in wonder at its beauty and thus give praise, unknowingly, to the Lord of the House; by being a true monk I may cause others to wish to train themselves that they may *know* the Lord of the House and become truly free.

To this end I must put forth Right Effort. The lotus puts forth seeds to grow more lotus plants; a monk makes an effort to exhibit the Truth by keeping the Precepts so that others may seek the Lord of the House also. By being thus single-minded in our efforts, both I and the lotus will for ever exhibit Right Mindfulness and not be distracted from our true purpose.

What is our true purpose? It is to show the Lord in everything we do, say and think. Who is the Lord of the House? I am not the Lord of the House but there is nothing in me that is not of the Lord of the House. The lotus is not the Lord of the House but there is nothing in it that is not of the Lord of the House. Both the lotus and I and you are the Lord of the House and we must not usurp the position of the Lord of the House. This is Right Concentration.

I must warn the trainees to guard their thoughts and, above all, not to let the worm of doubt get at their faith. By the time lying and deceit have appeared the spiritual plant is in grave danger: already its root and stem are diseased. Always they must keep up their meditation; always they must keep the Precepts.

The lotus blossom does not pull its roots out of the mud to get to the Lord of the House; it is content to drink in his life-giving sun that it may strengthen its stem and roots and be fruitful and multiply. I must stay for ever in meditation so that, by so doing, I may bathe eternally in the fountain of the Lord's love and wisdom thus causing others to wish to do the same. I must stay in the world as if in the sky, thus I may show the Lord's love and wisdom to all beings. Heaven is indeed a beautiful place but I will not enter it until I have united it with this world in which I live.

PLATE XL:– HEAVEN AND EARTH ARE ONE.

It is the morning of the 22nd. of January. I am again in the Buddha Land. Yesterday evening I was there for a brief moment and it was as if the sea were about to engulf it. It had already almost reached the little house which enclosed the fountain when I realised that the only person who could stop it was me. I grasped my will with all my might and commanded it to recede and it did so just a little. Now this morning, as I meditate, I watch it recede further and further leaving more and more of the shore exposed until there is absolutely no water left and the sea bed is exposed. The lotus blossoms withdraw their stems as the water level sinks, drawing them deeper and deeper into the earth until the blossoms rest on the newly-revealed ground. The beings in them step off onto the earth and mingle with the people of the world, appearing as ordinary beings, whether human or animal. The fountain, which had seemed almost to dry up last night, now flows freely again–and heaven and earth are one.

Herein lies another use of the five columns of light. It is by means of the first that I may *know* the Buddha Land; by means of the second I become fit to enter it; by means of the third I may *know* that the whole universe *is* the Buddha Land; by means of the fourth I am given the love and strength to combine them in the fifth.

A new perspective is obtained by harmonising body and mind. Without that harmony heaven is engulfed in the waters of delusion, which is the negative term for the waveless sea, and the seemingly endless cycle of aimless and meaningless births and deaths continues; men and women become more frustrated and angry as time goes by, die in bitterness and confusion and are reborn to the same endless cycle. And all they have to do is harmonise body and mind to be free for ever! Along with the meditation and sincerity of purpose I have described, here is the way in which I must live if I would maintain that harmony.

Each of my organs must be well cared for as individuals and nourished appropriately, taking into account that my mental states correspond to the amount of tension placed on various organs. For example, if I am depressed, my lungs need love and their correct food and I must offer that which depresses them up the first column of light.

If my body and mind would stay in harmony I must give it the correct amount of rest, rising with the sun, going to sleep eight hours before sunrise. I must cleanse it with love and caress it with adequately warm clothing. "Your body deserves love and respect for it is by its agency that Truth is practised and the Buddha's power exhibited," says Dōgen. It is not to be whipped, scourged, tortured or ill-treated: it is not by such means that a being may enter into the knowledge of the Lord of the House; it is wrong to try to take heaven by storm. This body is of the Lord; how could he be pleased with a being that damaged it in any way? It was given to me to love and to cherish, not to abuse.

But there is much more to abuse of the body than physical violence. If I would live in the world as if in the sky I must not become a cannibal and rape the bodies of animals for the sake of gratifying an untrained palate. When meat is eaten my skhandas cry out in agony for they know the pain of the being that died; they are one with it. It is grievous to harm any living thing, even a green leaf, for it too is of the Lord, but it is criminal to cause deliberate physical pain to the Lord—and the killing of animals does just that.

If I would retain the harmony of body and mind I may not indulge in sexuality. The purpose of meditation is to free beings from the trammels of earth so that they may penetrate heaven; in it one offers up everything one has, returning it to the Lord for it is, indeed, His. It is for this reason that the harmonisation of body and mind does not usually occur until a being is over forty years of age. The sex act forces life downwards and leaves those who participate therein empty and flaccid; true meditation turns life upwards to the Lord, leaving those who practice it truly full and joyful. The sex act causes desire for sex to become stronger and stronger and results in delusion, inaccuracy of memory, loss of intelligence and obsession. Meditation results in peace of mind, accuracy of memory, high intelligence and true freedom. When one is young it is difficult to believe this and so much grief and despair is experienced and the harmonisation of body and mind does not take place until the obsessions of youth have been overcome. He who would harmonise body and mind needs to be celibate in both *body and mind* for at least three years. True marriage, in which sex is not *indulged*, will *not* cause a being to be unable to harmonise body and mind once the fires of youth have cooled, but he who *gratifies* his lusts can only look for an endless cycle of births, old age, disease and death; the Lord will not grant him harmony of body and mind. Nor must I satisfy myself through masturbation; the body is the temple of the Lord: I must not rape the Lord at the temple gate. The *only* use of sex is the procreation of children.

Sexual indulgence and lust are the desecration of the Lord. It is for the purpose of usurping the Lord's power that the sex act is used in witchcraft. The sex act binds one being to another; by returning life to the Lord, instead of constantly snatching and wasting it by constantly indulging oneself, a being becomes one again *with* the Lord. Sexual indulgence is the laying waste of love, the despoiling of heaven, a wasting of the Lord's gifts. Pills and devices that enable beings to so indulge themselves create more and more tensions in the organs until disease develops which may prevent all hope of the harmonisation of body and mind in this life-time.

If I would keep the harmonisation of body and mind I must guard my eyes and ears from that which causes tensions in my body and if, in the course of living in the world, this is not always possible, I must not allow what I see and hear to affect me; instead I must offer all such things up the first column to the Lord so that they may be cleansed in his love.

Beings who have not yet experienced the harmonisation of body and mind must do this in pure faith for they do not yet know *for themselves* the certainty of the existence of the five columns. A being who has experienced the Penetration of Heaven kenshō knows of the first column and so can offer everything to the Lord with a measure of certainty as well as faith in the other four columns; a being who has experienced the Harmonisation of Body and Mind kenshō can offer everything to the Lord in absolute certainty and is beyond faith whilst being ignorant in many matters. Thus a being can only use as much as he knows *for certain* for himself; for the rest he must use faith.

What are these sights and sounds that I should not see and hear? Theatrical, television and other shows that pretend to entertain by showing the killing, maiming and insulting of other beings or which indulge in lewd, deluded and questionable humour; doubts that are caused either by books or raised by those who have not yet raised the seed of Bodhi within themselves and are sceptical, either out of fear or jealousy, of those who have. Such sights and words are to be absolutely avoided if the heart, small intestine, bladder and kidneys are to remain at peace. Should sights and sounds in real life cause them dis-ease, again these sights and sounds must immediately be offered up to be cleansed by the Lord in the second column. Meditation is the key to every situation.

I must avoid unclean and polluted air if I would have peace in my lungs; I will allow no anaesthetic to be used upon them nor will I permit any drug to dull the exquisite joy of these my senses. Thus, by not indulging the six senses of smell, taste, words, hearing, touch and sight, the harmony of my body and mind will be unimpaired until my work is done and the Lord takes back that which is His own. Thus will I live in the world as if in the sky.

PLATE XLI:– NOTHING MATTERS.

It does not matter if anyone who reads this book believes what I have written. I have simply written down an account of my own training during the past year and the way in which I shall conduct it for myself in the future. It is not *my* problem that I am good for others; if they wish to follow my way then they are free to do so; if they wish to go their own way they are free to do so. Shakyamuni Buddha told his disciples, "Do not believe anything I have said because you have heard it from me; when you have proved it true for yourselves *then* you can believe it absolutely." This is a teaching that I put into practice years ago, refusing to teach anything I had read in any book on Buddhism, or any Scripture, until I personally *knew* with my whole being that it was true for *me*. Only by so doing could I live at peace with myself.

It is not the *Lord's* problem that *He* is good for beings as I found out in the darkness when faced with the abyss. The Lord is the Lord and we are free to return to Him or to turn away from Him; either way it is not His problem.

It is not my problem if others get hurt by my teaching for there is no way in which I can *really* hurt them; 'no doer is there who does the deed nor is there one who feels the fruit.' All hurt is illusion and in ratio to the size of the egocentric self; whilst in duality there are pain and pleasure, good and evil; when body and mind are harmonised they both vanish. Trainees come and go, they train themselves or they do not according to their personal bent; if they are truly my disciples they try to follow my teaching; if they are not they go their own way. Either way it is not my problem nor is it the Lord's.

I must not worry if I become sick although it is my duty to properly care for the Lord's property, my body. Since there is neither birth nor death in the Lord there are but times when a being is seen and when it is not seen and when it is seen again in differing shapes and colours. Appearing and disappearing, form and emptiness are but manifestations of the Lord; appearing here, disappearing there, the Lord remains eternally, unseen, unheard, untouched, unsmelt, untasted save by those who have truly looked for He is indeed there for all to see, hear, touch, smell and taste and, above all, to KNOW. 'The means of training are thousandfold but PURE Zazen must be done.' The means of finding Him are so very simple; all we have to do is sit down with an open mind.

I must not hold on to what I have seen during this past year nor must I hold on to not holding on to it. I must not say that it did not happen, as some people here would have me say, for that would be to deny that void is form; nor may I say that anything I have seen is to be found in a tangible place for that would be to deny that form is void. I must not hold on to the fact that I exist, nor to the fact that I do not exist; such arguments as these theories engender are for philosophers to waste their time with; the photograph of my dead mother is but an empty imprint on paper of that which is already something else; if I place it in the fire that which was paper will immediately become ashes—where is there any photograph, where my mother?—both took form, became void and took form again. I KNOW that nothing matters and that I must not hold on to nothing mattering. 'Thus shall ye think of all this fleeting world, a star at dawn, a bubble in a stream, a child's laugh, a phantasm, a dream.'

To live beyond duality may seem cold to the dualistic mind—I can assure such a mind that to live beyond the opposites is anything but cold. To bathe in the Lord's fountain is to be washed thoroughly and intimately with pure love. To live beyond the opposites is to *know* that, no matter what a being has done in the past, he is, and always was, immaculate. Living beyond the opposites eliminates the problem of labels that the world puts on others; it is *knowing* that he whom the world labels a criminal is immaculate in the sight of the Lord; it is knowing that she whom the world dubs a prostitute has equal rights with the head of state before the Lord. They are not the Lord and the Lord is *all* of them. For centuries we have usurped the Lord's prerogative, setting up our petty opinions. Still the Lord waits in all-embracing silence. Who can fathom such love? I bathed in the Lord's fountain and I cannot even conceive of the depth of that love. I can only tell others of it and hope and pray that they may know it too before they die.

In the darkest place the Lord gave me all of the teaching and in the lightest place His teaching remains the same. During my kenshō in 1963 He gave me the same teaching and He will give it me again at the hour of death—NOTHING MATTERS—what a magnificent, peace-bringing teaching this is. Last summer I wrote the essence of the teaching I had received during those early months into a mantra; I write it again here for any who may find it useful:—

I am *Glad* that I Became a Monk.

The Treasure House exists; when the Lord of the House permits me to hold the Jewel I must do so with awe and reverence. I must hold it so that each facet is distinct. I should not show this Jewel idly to those still caught in fame and gain, who may consider or weigh its worth, but I show it anyway.

Nothing matters;

Mindfulness is all.

The Scriptures must be taken *literally* for they were obtained at death's door;

Never come too close nor put yourself too far away from anything.

If life comes there is only life;

If death comes there is only death;

I step off into death when my purpose for living ceases;

I step off into life when my purpose for living emerges;

My purpose for living is to be a monk so now is not the time to die.

It is sufficient for *me* just to *BE* a monk.

Although being careful of other's training, I can not do it for them; they and I make and carry our own karma; they must find their *own* purpose for living.

To be a live monk I must *know* the harmony of body and mind;

The body will not cease from sickness until the mind ceases from evil.

The Lord of the House says, "If you wish," when I make my choices;

The consequences are not his problem.

If I am to be a monk I must unceasingly heed the Lord of the House;

When the Lord of the House gives you his teaching listen attentively and respectfully and, quickly, loudly, reverently and obediently, say "YES."

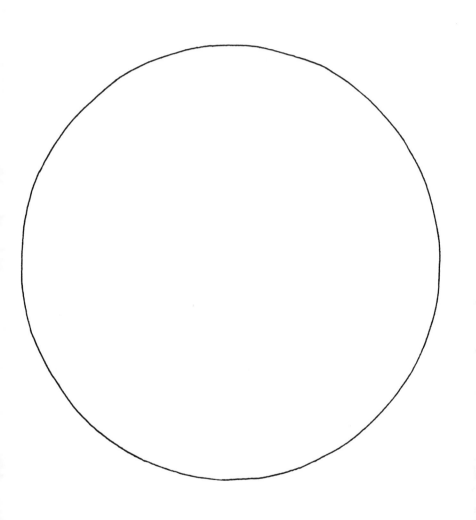

PLATE XLII:– THE LORD OF THE HOUSE.

The Lord of the House remains eternally in meditation, in eternal training; unmoved, unhasting, silent.
All creatures are born, die and are born again–none
impedes the Lord's work. Like the Buddhas and Patriarchs of old, the Lord helps and teaches at all times
just by being the Lord. He, She, It is not a being and is
not not a being. He has no specific gender, no specific
form. He is not emptiness and He is not not emptiness.
We are born here, die there, born again to joy or
sorrow accordingly as we have cleansed ourselves from
our karmic impregnations–the Lord waits and waits
eternally. Why? *I* am not a god. It is enough for me to
know the Lord of the House, more I neither ask nor
seek. The Lord of the House has no beginning and no
end, no past and no future. I am not Him and He is
all of me.

For centuries people have caused Buddhism to
suffer under the belief that it was a way of life and not
a religion. This was because they feared saying the
Truth lest they set up a god to be worshipped. The
Lord is not a god and He is not not a god. He is not a
saviour; and if, at the moment of death, a person can
embrace infinity instead of his own delusions, he is
immediately united with the Lord. At all times we are
free to unite with, or turn away from, the Lord. If you
would know the Lord know that the means of training
are thousandfold but PURE Zazen *must* be done.
Through Zazen we are immediately united with the
Lord; together with him we go out into emptiness, into
form and again into emptiness.......

PLATE XLIII:– NOT EMPTINESS, NOT FULLNESS, NOT CIRCULAR, NOT SPATIAL.

It is the morning of the twenty-sixth of January. Within luminescent darkness floats a great ball of pink and gold light. It contains the fifth light column. It pulses with life, turning in upon itself, for ever changing. The luminescent darkness takes the shape of a great beast, blacker than the darkness–the beast of fear. I feel neither fear nor elation, joy nor sorrow. The beast dissolves into the luminescent darkness which is limitless space. The ball of pink and gold moves ceaselessly, unhindered by the shapes the darkness takes. They are not Its problem. I ask for Kōzan and Daizui; they come in. I ask what I should do next and am told through Daizui to be very still. We wait. I ask again, "What should I do? I am willing to do *anything* you wish." I am told, "Go on." I go on. I gasp as I am enfolded in the ball of light.This is my father's face before I was conceived; I enter the Womb of the Lord. The Womb draws me to its centre, dark and light simultaneously. I *am* its centre; the new-born Buddha stands within its centre, one hand pointing up, the other down. I am infused with that which brings neither ecstasy nor grief–it *is* as it should *be*. First I see the ball of light, then I am within it and then I see the new-born Buddha standing within it. 'Back to the origin, back to the source'–the ninth Ox-Herding Picture; It floats in space, without beginning, without end, without past, without future.

Whilst waiting for the Lord's Will I see beings coming and going within the ball of light throughout which moves a red ribbon of light like the red lines of the Ketchimyaku and Shishō. The ribbon can take any shape or form, for ever turning, for ever moving. The beings are upon the red ribbon, here appearing as human, there as animal, god, insect, rising, falling, ever moving, never resting, nothing excluded. The Light of the Lord of the House, the heart-mind, irradiates the infinity of space—within its centre I may not say that it is empty; I may not say that it is not empty. It is unstained, immaculate; I am not It, It is all of me; thus form is void and void is form.

When I allow external things to influence me endless space takes on endless colours and forms that titillate or terrify my senses; when I am still these shapes, which are the shapes of fear and the negative side of desire, have no means of manifesting themselves. Desire and craving are but respectable names for fear; I must remember this. They shall not enslave me again.

Nothing is born, nothing dies. We shape our fears from emptiness and unto emptiness they must return. The only seemingly *real emptiness* is fear; the Lord enfolds emptiness and is not empty nor is not not empty. Within the Lord all senses, form, thought, all things, cease and nothing ceases; there are neither old age nor death and there is no ceasing of old age and death as the world understands them. One undertakes meditation when one is young so as to make some sense out of life or to escape death. The Lord promises us small presents so that He may give us our true inheritance. Life and death, body and mind, fall away naturally for they no longer apply. A few days ago there was a return of my illness; a month ago it would have mattered; now it is as it should be—there is no *extinction* of old age and death. If life comes there is only life; if death comes there is only death. All acceptance is the key that unlocks the gateless gate. Within this place there is no suffering, no coming, no going, no ceasing, no way. There is only endless training, appearing here, disappearing there, going in and out, always BECOMING Buddha. The Wheel turns endlessly, the Precepts and the Eightfold Path are far behind as tools used by a carpenter are put away when a building is completed but never discarded lest they be needed again.

The Wheel of the Law, the Wheel of Becoming—it is I who turn the Wheel of the Law—the Wheel of the Law, the heart-mind, the Lord of the House and I are one. I am not Them; They are *all* of me; form *is* void; void *is* form—say not void, say not form. Om, to the One who leaps beyond all fear; Awakened, awakened, I *have* awakened. O merciful One, compassionate One, of daring ones the most joyous, hail! Thou hast the Wheel within Thine hand, hail! Thou Who hast the lotus, hail! Hail to Thee Who art the root of eternity! Hail to Thee Who art all compassion, hail!

POSTWORD.

In the course of our discussions during the preparation of this book, Kennett Rōshi asked me to reiterate several points of particular importance to readers.
1. The meditation described in this book was undertaken solely with the thought of cleaning up her life in the face of imminent death. It was *NOT* done to cure illness nor to have religious visions. *PLEASE* do not meditate for selfish reasons; meditate, if you do, to find the way to change your life, the way to make it into an offering to the Lord of the House and to all beings.
2. To have a kenshō experience, or *any* religious experience, is neither the purpose nor the end of religious training. The religious life is endless; there is always a new beginning; always there is the going on, always *becoming* Buddha. Thus, the question of whether one "is enlightened" or not simply does not arise in the true trainee's mind, and the mind of the Zen Master and that of the beginner are one. Do not get stuck with immaculacy, nor the abyss, nor ecstasy, not even the Lord of the House—*all is* a kaleidoscopic tapestry of moving rest. The first time one realizes this with one's whole being is often the moment of the first type of kenshō described in this book. But if you do not realize and live it every moment thereafter, what use is that first realization? If you continue the life of religion and deepen it thereafter, this understanding becomes the touch-stone of your life, the center of your being from which you go in and out to do that which is good for all living things. When it is

right to return to this and dwell in it, then it is there, within you, the *true home* of your whole being. And when it is time to go forth again, whether to serve the Buddha's creatures or to pass beyond this understanding to another one, as yet darkly veiled, there is just the going on, going on—always with faith and a smile in your heart, and always with the humility of knowing that this is but the smallest part of the Lord's Truth.

Daizui MacPhillamy

APPENDIX A:–
THE FLOW OF THE BREATH
DURING MEDITATION.

If you wish to harmonise body and mind it is absolutely *imperative* that you study the Zazen Rules in *detail*.

First, and foremost, keep your eyes open.

Second, control mind function, will, consciousness, memory, perception and understanding–if any one of these is allowed to predominate the balance and rhythm of the meditation will be upset and you will get nowhere. Be alert enough so that, every time one or the other of these conditions begins to appear, you can control it; awareness is the key-word here.

Third, it does not *matter* whether you are sitting or lying down although the latter should only be used *constantly* if you are sick; laziness must be guarded against at all times; right effort is *always* required.

Fourth, do not worry about thoughts coming and going; just do *not* grab at them and do *not* push them away; watch them flow by naturally and do not be concerned with, or interested in, them.

Fifth, take two or three deep breaths when you *start* to meditate and then allow the breathing to become natural; do *not* try to make it different from what is *natural breathing for you.*

Because of the mistakes made with regard to the last mentioned this appendix is chiefly concerned with *how* to take those two or three deep breaths.

Shakyamuni Buddha, after trying many harsh disciplines and finding them uesless, decided to try the method of breathing He had used as a child of seven.

He was *immediately* successful in His attempts to reach enlightenment; He succeeded *that very same night*. Every small child knows how to meditate properly; it is only after we have "educated" it that its body and mind become separated. This was just as true of Shakyamuni Buddha as it is of us. This separation of body and mind can be precipitated by many things *besides* "education;" *anything*, in fact, that instils greed for worldly gain through competitiveness (the main cause of the disharmony of body and mind and its resulting tensions which ultimately lead to ill-health). Constantly quarrelling parents, or parents that do not make a secure home for their children, can cause the separation a lot earlier than the age of seven. This being so, he who would meditate properly must set up the breathing pattern that he used as a child. Here is how it is done.

Study Fig. A carefully. The breath originates in the hara; an area roughly triangular in shape with its base in the area of the navel and its apex at the base of the sternum, the sides roughly corresponding to the sides of the rib cage; this is shown in Fig. A as 'Body, 1.' One should *not* count breaths when meditating; one should *follow the course* that the breath takes. Most people breathe without thinking about it but the meditator must *consciously*, at the *beginning* of each meditation, as well as at any time that he *loses* his awareness during that meditation, *follow* each breath thus:— inhalation starts at the base of the spine and continues up the spine to the crown of the head; exhalation starts at the crown of the head and continues down the front of the body to the pubic area where inhalation takes over at the base of the spine. Thus the breath goes in a circle, inhalation up the back of the body and exhalation down the front, and this circular breathing is the turning of the Wheel of the Law. In *meditation* this fol-

187

lowing of the breath is done consciously *two or three times* so that the breathing pattern may be established both physically and psychologically and then it must be *left behind* and the breathing allowed to settle *naturally* into the rhythm that is right for the individual.

When one finds that this type of breathing is so natural that it is second-nature, one will notice that there are tiny fractions of time, called 'apertures' in the breath, between inhalation and exhalation. If a person has been able to learn how *not* to be distracted by his thoughts he will be still enough to hear the still, small voice, the voice of the Lord of the House, during these tiny intervals: it is by means of listening to these that body and mind once again enter into harmony—thus the place where exhalation takes over from inhalation is marked as 'Mind, 2' on Fig. A. 1 and 2 are the two most obvious 'apertures' in the breathing and are the first ones of which a meditator becomes aware. After a time he will discover himself asking questions at 1 and hearing the answers at 2 (see Fig. 2, Verse 2). This is spoken of freely by Keizan Zenji in the Denkōroku. Incidentally, this is how a person works on a kōan in Rinzai Zen although I have, as yet, never seen it talked about in print. The kōan is asked at 1 and answered at 2; with the constant asking of a kōan, what is heard and known at 1 and 2 becomes clearer and clearer in the meditator's mind until body and mind once more briefly harmonise and the Penetration of Heaven kenshō results. As more kōans are worked on so the other kenshōs *may* be experienced and the harmonisation becomes permanent. It is important to remember that enlightenment, or understanding, is not obtained piecemeal; every kenshō contains the *whole* of enlightenment. 'When minute infinitesimally small becomes; when large, it transcends all dimension, space,' says the

Hōkyozammai—but the small one is still a kenshō—and there are plenty more kenshōs where that one came from!

When a person has become good at meditating in this way, which is nothing other than sitting quietly as the Zazen Rules state, he will find that he can hear the still, small voice in other places, first at 3 on Fig. A and then at 4. When he is good at this the still, small voice, his true nature, will take over from the voice of his egocentric-ego—the rôles that these two have played since the meditator suffered the disharmony of body and mind as a child will be reversed and then genuine spiritual progress is possible. The Christians call this state 'having conversations with God;' the Buddhist calls it the harmonisation of body and mind—it is explained elaborately in the Goi theory of Tōzan. The Sandōkai should be studied deeply in connection with Figs. A through E.

As meditation continues to deepen, the apertures in Fig. A become more numerous, see Fig. C, and the resulting kenshōs are correspondingly deeper until, in Fig. D, every aperture is used and the kenshō becomes a long and permanent experience—AND THERE ARE STILL MORE KENSHOS AFTER THIS ONE—it is *still* only the tip of the iceberg. Fig. B shows the Christian version of Fig. A and Fig. E, the Preparation for Death cycle, death occurring when the breath has reached the 'mind' position although exhalation still occurs.

Understand that *none* of the above can take place until the *involvement* in the *noise* of the human brain dies down; a person who is constantly chasing after his own thoughts and getting involved with them will be too busy to *hear* the Lord of the House!

Sometimes blockages in the *flow* of the breath seem to occur and the meditator becomes very tense in the shoulder area, 3, Fig. A. This is because of old opinions, ideas, fears, notions, etc. to which the person is clinging. The tension in this area can become so painful that it can only be relieved, and meditation continued, by the use of the kyosaku and this is its *rightful* purpose. Such use is called massage, not beating; this should be clearly understood and the kyosaku should be used at *no* other time. It is *not* an instrument of punishment. When a person has learned how to pass all things of a problematical nature up the second column of light, 3 on Fig. E, the tensions do not build up and the kyosaku becomes unnecessary.

Each of the columns of light correspond to 1, 2, 3, 4 and 5 on Fig. E and Plates XXVII-XLIII should be studied in conjunction with it and this appendix.

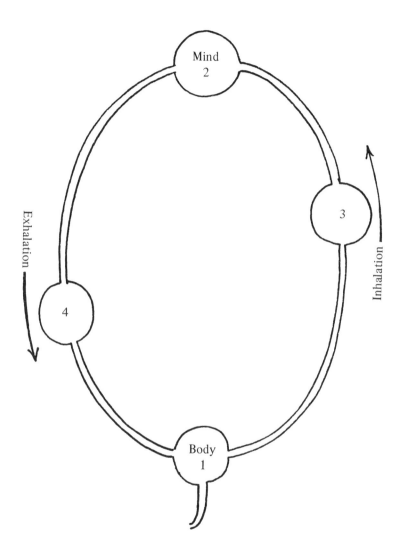

Fig. A. How to follow the circulation of the breath.

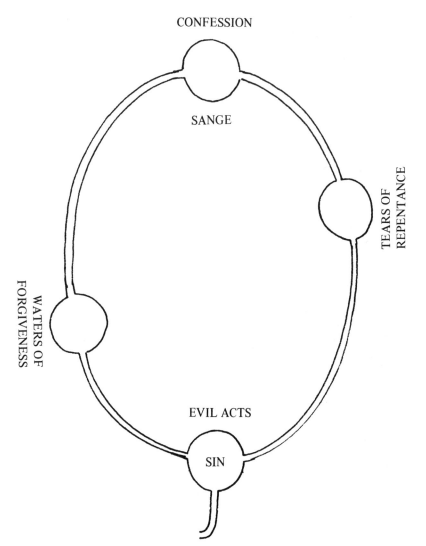

Fig. B. Act of Utter Contrition seen as preparation for kenshō. This cycle is also sometimes called the Fullness of Life, or Preparation for Death, kenshō.

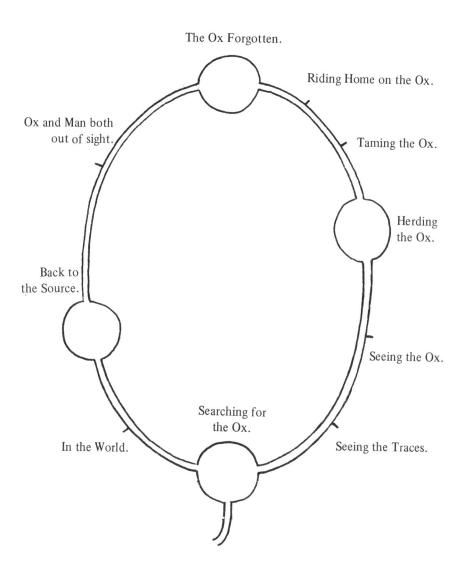

Fig. C. Positions of the Ox-Herding Pictures in the breath apertures at time of Penetration of Heaven kenshō.

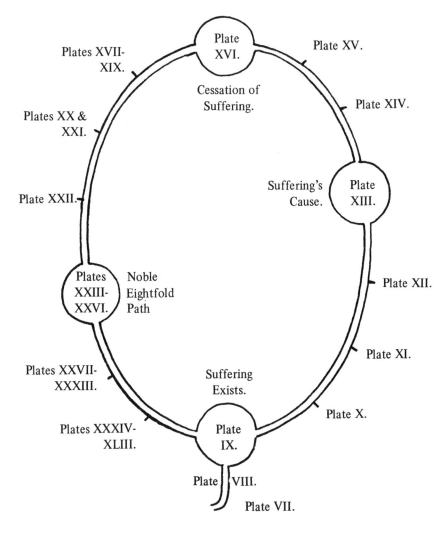

Fig. D. The arrangement of the apertures between inhalation and exhalation of the breath for the
Harmonisation of Body and Mind kenshō.

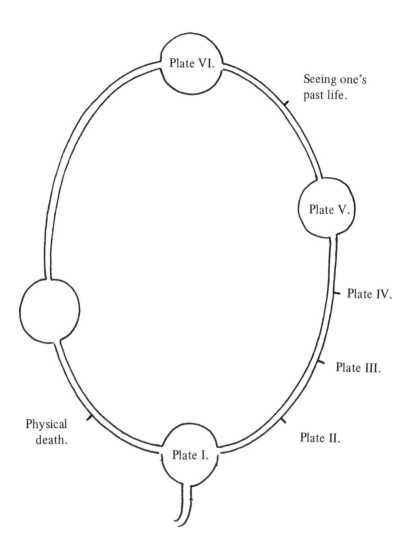

Fig. E. Preparation for Death cycle, or kenshō, leading to a peaceful death.

APPENDIX B:– THE LIFE OF THE HASIDIM.

In this appendix and the one following, we present works from other religious traditions which may be of interest to the reader for comparison with the text of this book. Here we reprint "The Life of the Hasidim," a work from the Judaic tradition found in *The Legend of the Baal-Shem* by Martin Buber, translated by Maurice Friedman, © 1955 by Harper & Row Publishers, Inc., by permission of the publisher. It is obvious to me from reading this exquisite writing that religious experiences such as those described in this book are not the "property" of any tradition. They transcend all limitations of doctrine, arising directly from That from which all doctrines come. The intuitively religious way of life has been led by people of all centuries, nations, and races; anyone, in fact, can lead it if he or she is willing to do so completely. We have also encountered similar passages in the works of some of the Christian mystics and in some incompletely-translated sections of the Buddhist sutras. It is our hope to include selections from these works in the next edition of this book.

Daizui MacPhillamy

THE LIFE OF THE HASIDIM.[1]

Hitlahavut: Ecstasy

Hitlahavut is "the burning," the ardour of ecstasy.

A fiery sword guards the way to the tree of life. It scatters into sparks before the touch of hitlahavut, whose light finger is more powerful than it. To hitlahavut the path is open, and all bounds sink before its boundless step. The world is no longer its place: it is the place of the world.

Hitlahavut unlocks the meaning of life. Without it even heaven has no meaning and no being. "If a man has fulfilled the whole of the teaching and all the commandments, but has not had the rapture and the burning, when he dies and passes beyond, paradise is opened to him, but because he has not felt rapture in the world, he also does not feel it in paradise."

Hitlahavut can appear at all places and at all times. Each hour is its footstool and each deed its throne. Nothing can stand against it, nothing hold it down; nothing can defend itself against its might, which raises everything corporeal to spirit. He who is in it is in holiness. "He can speak idle words with his mouth, yet the teaching of the Lord is in his heart at this hour; he can pray in a whisper, yet his heart cries out in his breast; he can sit in a community of men, yet

---

1. Followers of the mystical Judaic tradition known as Hasidism founded by Rabbi Israel ben Eliezer in eastern Europe in the 18th century, A. D.

he walks with God: mixing with the creatures yet secluded from the world." Each thing and each deed is thus sanctified. "When a man attaches himself to God, he can allow his mouth to speak what it may speak and his ear to hear what it may hear, and he will bind the things to their higher root."

Repetition, the power which weakens and discolours so much in human life, is powerless before ecstasy, which catches fire again and again from precisely the most regular, most uniform events. Ecstasy overcame one zaddik[2] in reciting the Scriptures, each time that he reached the words, "And God spoke." A Hasidic wise man who told this to his disciples added to it, "But I think also: if one speaks in truth and one receives in truth, then one word is enough to uplift the whole world and to purge the whole world from sin." To the man in ecstasy the habitual is eternally new. A zaddik stood at the window in the early morning light and trembling cried, "A few hours ago it was night and now it is day—God brings up the day!" And he was full of fear and trembling. He also said, "Every creature should be ashamed before the Creator: were he perfect, as he was destined to be, then he would be astonished and awakened and inflamed because of the renewal of the creature at each time and in each moment."

But hitlahavut is not a sudden sinking into eternity: it is an ascent to the infinite from rung to rung. To find God means to find the way without end. The Hasidim saw the "world to come" in the image of this way, and they never called that world a Beyond. One of the pious saw a dead master in a dream. The latter told him that from the hour of his death he went each day from world to world. And the world which yesterday was stretched out above his gaze as heaven is

---

2. The Hasidic rabbi or teacher.

to-day the earth under his foot; and the heaven of to-day is the earth of to-morrow. And each world is purer and more beautiful and more profound than the one before.

The angels rest in God, but the holy spirits go forward in God. "The angel is one who stands, and the holy man is one who travels on. Therefore the holy man is higher than the angel."

Such is the way of ecstasy. If it appears to offer an end, an arriving, an attaining, an acquiring, it is only a final no, not a final yes: it is the end of constraint, the shaking off of the last chains, the liberation which is lifted above everything earthly. "When man moves from strength to strength and ever upward and upward until he comes to the root of all teaching and all command, to the I of God, the simple unity and boundlessness—when he stands there, then all the wings of command and law sink down and are as if destroyed. For the evil impulse is destroyed since he stands above it."

"Above nature and above time and above thought"—thus is he called who is in ecstasy. He has cast off all sorrow and all that is oppressive. "Sweet suffering, I receive you in love," said a dying zaddik, and Rabbi Susya cried out amazed when his hand slipped out of the fire in which he had placed it, "How coarse Susya's body has become that it is afraid of fire." The man of ecstasy rules life, and no external happening that penetrates into his realm can disturb his inspiration. It is told of a zaddik that when the holy meal of the teaching prolonged itself till morning, he said to his disciples, "We have not stepped into the limits of the day, rather the day has stepped into our limits, and we need not give way before it."

In ecstasy all that is past and that is future draws near to the present. Time shrinks, the line between the eternities disappears, only the moment lives, and the moment is eternity. In its undivided light appears all that was and all that will be, simple and composed. It is there as a heart-beat is there, and becomes perceptible like it.

The Hasidic legend has much to tell of those wonderful ones who remembered their earlier forms of existence, who were aware of the future as of their own breath, who saw from one end of the earth to the other and felt all the changes that took place in the world as something that happened to their own bodies. All this is not yet that state in which hitlahavut has overcome the world of space and time. We can perhaps learn something of this latter state from two simple anecdotes which supplement each other. It is told of one master that he had to look at a clock during the hour of withdrawal in order to keep himself in this world; and of another that when he wished to observe individual things, he had to put on spectacles in order to restrain his spiritual vision, "for otherwise he saw all the individual things of the world as one."

But the highest rung which is reported is that in which the withdrawn one transcends his own ecstasy. When a disciple once remarked that a zaddik had "grown cold" and censored him for it, he was instructed by another, "There is a very high holiness; if one enters it, one becomes detached from all being and can no longer become inflamed." Thus ecstasy completes itself in its own suspension.

At times it expresses itself in an action, consecrates it and fills it with holy meaning. The purest form—that in which the whole body serves the aroused soul and in which each of the soul's risings and bendings creates a visible symbol corresponding to it, allowing one image of enraptured meaning to emerge out of a thousand waves of movement—is the dance. It is told of the dancing of one zaddik, "His foot was as light as that of a four-your-old child. And among all who saw his holy dancing, there was not one in whom the holy turning was not accomplished, for in the hearts of all who saw he worked both weeping and rapture in one." Or the soul lays hold of the voice of a man and makes it sing what the soul has experienced in the heights, and the voice does not know what it does. Thus one zaddik stood in prayer in the "days of awe" (New Year and the Day of Atonement) and sang new melodies, "wonder of wonder, that he had never heard and that no human ear had ever heard, and he did not know at all what he sang and in what way he sang, for he was bound to the upper world."

But the truest life of the man of ecstasy is not among men. It is said of one master that he behaved like a stranger, according to the words of David the King: A sojourner am I in the land. "Like a man who comes from afar, from the city of his birth. He does not think of honours nor of anything for his own welfare; he only thinks about returning home to the city of his birth. He can possess nothing, for he knows: That is alien, and I must go home." Many walk in solitude, in "the wandering." Rabbi Susya used to stride about in the woods and sing songs of praise with so great ardour "that one would almost say that he was out of his mind." Another was only to be found in the streets and gardens and groves. When his father-in-law reproved him for this, he answered with the parable of the hen who hatched out goose eggs, "And when she saw her children swimming about on the surface of the water, she ran up and down in consternation seeking help for the unfortunate ones; and did not understand that this was their whole life to them: to roam on the surface of the water."

There are still more profoundly solitary ones whose hitlahavut, for all that, is not yet fulfilled. They become "unsettled and fugitive." They go into exile in order "to suffer exile with the Shekina." It is one of the basic conceptions of the Kabbala that the Shekina, the "indwelling" presence of God, endlessly wanders in exile, separated from her "lord," and that she will be reunited with him only in the hour of redemption. So these men of ecstasy wander over the earth, dwelling in the silent distances of God's exile, companions of the universal and holy happening of existence. The man who is detached in this way is the friend of God, "as a stranger is the friend of another stranger on account of their strangeness on earth." There are moments in which he sees the Shekina face to face in human form, as that zaddik saw it in the Holy Land "in the shape of a woman who weeps and laments over the husband of her youth."

But not only in faces out of the dark and in the silence of wandering does God give Himself to the soul afire with Him. Rather out of all the things of the earth His eye looks into the eye of him who seeks, and every being is the fruit in which He offers Himself to the yearning soul. Being is unveiled in the hand of the holy man. "The soul of him who longs very much for a woman and regards her many-coloured garment is not turned to its gorgeous material and its colours but to the splendour of the longed-for woman who is clothed in it. But the others see only the garment and no more. So he who in truth longs for and embraces God sees in all the things of the world only the strength and the pride of the Creator who lives in the things. But he who is not on this rung sees the things as separate from God."

This is the earthly life of hitlahavut which soars beyond all limits. It enlarges the soul to the all. It narrows the all down to nothing. A Hasidic master speaks of it in words of mystery, "The creation of heaven and of earth is the unfolding of something out of nothing, the descent of the higher into the lower. But the holy men who detach themselves from being and ever cleave to God see and comprehend Him in truth, as if there was now the nothing as before creation. They turn the something back into nothing. And this is the more wonderful: to raise up what is beneath. As it is written in the Gemara: The last wonder is greater than the first."

Avoda: Service

Hitlahavut is embracing God beyond time and space. Avoda is the service of God in time and space.

Hitlahavut is the mystic meal. Avoda is the mystic offering.

These are the poles between which the life of the holy man swings.

Hitlahavut is silent since it lies on the heart of God. Avoda speaks, "What am I and what is my life that I wish to offer you my blood and my fire?"

Hitlahavut is as far from avoda as fulfilment is from longing. And yet hitlahavut streams out of avoda as the finding of God from the seeking of God.

The Baal-Shem[3] told, "A king once built a great and glorious palace with numberless chambers, but only one door was opened. When the building was finished, it was announced that all princes should appear before the king who sat enthroned in the last of the chambers. But when they entered, they saw that there were doors open on all sides which led to winding

---

3. "The master of God's name;" a name given to Rabbi Israel ben Eliezer, founder of Hasidism.

passages in the distance, and there were again doors and again passages, and no end arose before the bewildered eyes. Then came the king's son and saw that all the labyrinth was a mirrored illusion, and he saw his father sitting in the hall before him."

The mystery of grace cannot be interpreted. Between seeking and finding lies the tension of a human life, indeed the thousandfold return of the anxious, wandering soul. And yet the flight of a moment is slower than the fulfilment. For God wishes to be sought, and how could he not wish to be found?

When the holy man brings ever new fire that the glowing embers on the altar of his soul may not be extinguished, God Himself says the sacrificial speech.

God rules man as He ruled chaos at the time of the infancy of the world. "And as when the world began to unfold and He saw that if it flowed further asunder it would no longer be able to return home to its roots, then he spoke, 'Enough!'—so it is that when the soul of man in its suffering rushes headlong, without direction, and evil becomes so mighty in it that it soon could no longer return home, then His compassion awakens, and he says, 'Enough!' "

But man too can say "Enough!" to the multiplicity within him. When he collects himself and becomes one, he draws near to the oneness of God—he serves his Lord. This is avoda.

It was said of one zaddik, "With him, teaching and prayer and eating and sleeping are all one, and he can raise the soul to its root."

All action bound in one and the infinite life enclosed in every action: this is avoda. "In all the deeds of man—speaking and looking and listening and going and remaining standing and lying down—the boundless is clothed."

From every deed an angel is born, a good angel or a bad one. But from half-hearted and confused deeds which are without meaning or without power, angels are born with twisted limbs or without a head or hands or feet.

When through all action the rays of the universal sun radiate and the light concentrates in every deed, this is service. But no special act is elected for this service. God wills that one serve Him in all ways.

"There are two kinds of love: the love of a man for his wife, which ought properly to express itself in secret and not where spectators are, for this love can only fulfil itself in a place secluded from the creatures; and the love for brothers and sisters and for children, which needs no concealment. Similarly, there are two kinds of love for God: the love through the teaching and prayer and the fulfilment of the commandments— this love ought properly to be consummated in silence and not in public, in order that it may not tempt one to glory and pride—and the love in the time in which one mixes with the creatures, when one speaks and hears, gives and takes with them, and yet in the secret of one's heart one cleaves to God and does not cease to think of Him. And this is a higher rung than that, and of it it is said, 'Oh, that thou wert as my brother that sucked on the breasts of my mother! When I should find thee without I would kiss thee; yea, and none would dispise me.' "

This is not to be understood, however, as if there were in this kind of service a cleavage between the earthly and the heavenly deed. Rather each motion of the surrendered soul is a vessel of holiness and of power. It is told of one zaddik that he had so sanctified all his limbs that each step of his feet wed worlds to one another. "Man is a ladder, placed on earth and touching heaven with its head. And all his gestures and affairs and speaking leave traces in the higher world."

Here the inner meaning of avoda is intimated, coming from the depths of the old Jewish secret teaching and illuminating the mystery of that duality of ecstasy and service, of having and seeking.

God has fallen into duality through the created world and its deed: into the being of God, Elohim, which is withdrawn from the creatures, and the presence of God, the Shekina, which dwells in things, wandering, straying, scattered. Only redemption will reunite the two in eternity. But it is given to the human spirit, through its service, to be able to bring the Shekina near to its source, to help it to enter it. And in this moment of home-coming, before it must again descend into the being of things, the whirlpool which rushes through the life of the stars becomes silent, the torches of the great devastation are extinguished, the whip in the hand of fate drops down, the world-pain pauses and listens: the grace of graces has appeared, blessing pours down out of infinity. Until the power of entanglement begins to drag down the Shekina and all becomes as before.

That is the meaning of service. Only the prayer that takes place for the sake of the Shekina truly lives. "Through his need and his want he knows the want of the Shekina, and he prays that the want of the Shekina will be satisfied and that through him, the praying man, the unification of God with His Shekina will take place." Man should know that his suffering comes from the suffering of the Shekina. He is "one of her limbs," and the stilling of her need is the only true stilling of his. "He does not think about the satisfaction of his needs, neither the lower nor the higher ones, that he might not be like him who cuts off the eternal plants and causes separation. Rather he does all for the sake of the want of the Shekina, and all will be resolved of itself, and his own suffering too will be stilled out of the stilling of the higher roots. For all, above and below, is one unity." "I am prayer," speaks the Shekina. A zaddik said, "Men think they pray before God, but it is not so, for prayer itself is divinity."

In the narrow room of self no prayer can thrive. "He who prays in suffering because of the melancholy which masters him and thinks that he prays in fear of God, or he who prays in joy because of the brightness of his mood and thinks he prays in love of God—his prayer is nothing at all. For this fear is only melancholy and this love is only empty joy."

It is told that the Baal-Shem once remained standing on the threshold of a house of prayer and did not want to enter. He spoke in aversion, "I cannot enter there. The house is full to the brim of teaching and prayer." And when his companions were astonished, because it appeared to them that there could be no greater praise than this, he explained to them, "During the day the people speak here words without true devotion, without love and compassion, words that have no wings. They remain between the walls, they squat on the floor, they grow layer by layer like decaying leaves until the decay has packed the house to overflowing and there is no longer room for me in there."

Prayer may be held down in two different ways: if it is spoken without inner intention and if the earlier deeds of the praying man lie spread out like a heavy cloud between him and heaven. The obstacle can only be overcome if the man grows upward into the sphere of ecstasy and purifies himself in its grace, or if another soul who is in ecstasy sets the fettered prayers free and carries them upward along with his own. Thus it is told of one zaddik that he stood for a long time silent and without movement during communal prayer and only then began himself to pray, "just as the tribe of Dan lay at the end of the camp and gathered all that was lost." His word became a garment to whose folds the prayers that were held below would cling and be borne upward. This zaddik used to say of prayer, "I bind myself with the whole of Israel, with those who are greater than I that through them my thoughts may ascend, and with those who are lesser than I that they may be uplifted through me."

But this is the mystery of community: not only do the lower need the higher, but the higher also need the lower. Here lies another distinction between the state of ecstasy and the state of service. Hitlahavut is the individual way and goal; a rope is stretched over the abyss, tied to two slender trees shaken by the storm: it is tread in solitude and dread by the foot of the venturer. Here there is no human community, neither in doubt nor in attainment. Service, however, is open to many souls in union. The souls bind themselves to one another for greater unity and might. There is a service that only the community can fulfil.

The Baal-Shem told a parable: "Some men stood under a very high tree. And one of the men had eyes to see. He saw that in the top of the tree stood a bird, glorious with genuine beauty. But the others did not see it. And a great longing came over the man to reach the bird and take it; and he could not go from there without the bird. But because of the height of the tree this was not in his power, and a ladder was not to be had. But because his longing was so overpowering he found a way. He took the men who stood around him and placed them on top of one another, each on the shoulder of a comrade. He, however, climbed to the top so that he reached the bird and took it. And although the men had helped him, they knew nothing of the bird and did not see it. But he, who knew it and saw it, would not have been able to reach it without them. If, moreover, the lowest of them had left his place, then those above would have fallen to the earth. 'And the Temple of the Messiah is called the bird's nest in the book Zohar.' "

But it is not as if only the zaddik's prayer is received by God or as if only this prayer is lovely in His eyes. No prayer is stronger in grace and penetrates in more direct flight through all the worlds of heaven than that of the simple man who does not know anything to say and only knows to offer God the unbroken promptings of his heart. God receives them as a king receives the singing of a nightingale in his gardens at twilight, a singing that sounds sweeter to him than the homage of the princes in his throne-room. The Hasidic legend cannot give enough examples of the favour that shines on the undivided person and of the power of his service. One of these we shall set down here.

A villager who year after year attended the prayer-house of the Baal-Shem in the "days of awe" had a boy who was dull in understanding and could not even learn the shape of the letters, let alone understand the holy words. The father did not take him to the city on the days of awe, for he knew nothing. Still when he was thirteen years old and of age to receive God's law, the father took him with him on the Day of Atonement that he might not eat something on the day of penance through lack of knowledge and understanding. Now the boy had a little whistle on which he always whistled during the time when he sat in the field and pastured the sheep and calves. He had brought it with him in his pocket without the father's knowing it. The boy sat in the prayer-house during the holy hours and did not know anything to say. But when the Mussaf prayer was begun, he spoke to his father,

"Father, I have my whistle with me, and I wish to play on it." Then the father was very disturbed and commanded him, "Take care that you do not do so." And he had to hold himself in. But when the Mincha prayer came, he spoke again, "Father, allow me now to take my whistle." When the father saw that his soul desired to whistle, he became angry and asked him, "Where do you keep it?" and when the boy showed him the place, he laid his hand on the pocket and held it over it from then on to guard the whistle. But the Neila prayer began, and the lights burned trembling in the evening, and the hearts burned like the lights, unexhausted by the long waiting. And through the house the eighteen benedictions strode once again, weary but erect. And the great confession returned for the last time and, before the evening descended and God judged, lay yet once more before the ark of the Lord, its forehead on the floor and its hands extended. Then the boy could no longer suppress his ecstasy; he tore the whistle from his pocket and let its voice powerfully resound. All stood startled and bewildered. But the Baal-Shem raised himself above them and spoke, "The judgement is suspended, and wrath is dispelled from the face of the earth."

Thus every service which proceeds from a simple or a unified soul is sufficient and complete. But there is a still higher one. For he who has ascended from avoda to hitlahavut and has submerged his will in it and receives his deed from it alone, has risen above every separate service. "Each zaddik has his special way of serving. But when the zadikkim contemplate their root and attain to the Nothing, then they can serve God on all rungs." Thus one of them said, "I stand before God as a messenger boy." For he had attained to completion and to the Nothing so that he no longer possessed any special way. "Rather he stood ready for all ways which God might show him, as a messenger boy stands ready for all that his master will command him." He who thus serves in perfection has conquered the primeval duality and has brought hitlahavut into the heart of avoda. He dwells in the kingdom of life, and yet all walls have fallen, all boundary-stones are uprooted, all separation is destroyed. He is the brother of the creatures and feels their glance as if it were his own, their step as if his own feet walked, their blood as if it flowed through his own body. He is the son of God and lays his soul anxiously and securely in the great hand beside all the heavens and earths and unknown worlds, and stands on the flood of the sea into which all his thoughts and the wanderings of all beings flow. "He makes his body the throne of life and life the throne of the spirit and the spirit the throne of the soul and the soul the throne of the light of God's glory, and the light streams round about him, and he sits in the midst of the light and trembles and rejoices."

Kavana: Intention

Kavana is the mystery of a soul directed to a goal.
Kavana is not will. It does not think of transplanting an image into the world of actual things, of making fast a dream as an object so that it may be at hand, to be experienced at one's convenience in satiating recurrence. Nor does it desire to throw the stone of action into the well of happening that its waters may for awhile become troubled and astonished, only to return then to the deep command of their existence, nor to lay a spark on the fuse that runs through the succession of the generations, that a flame may jump from age to age until it is extinguished in one of them without sign or leave-taking. Not this is Kavana's meaning, that the horses pulling the great wagon should feel one impulse

211

more or that one building more should be erected beneath the overfull gaze of the stars. Kavana does not mean purpose but goal.

But there are no *goals*, only *the goal*. There is only one goal that does not lie, that becomes entangled in no new way, only one into which all ways flow, before which no by-way can forever flee: redemption.

Kavana is a ray of God's glory that dwells in each man and means redemption.

This is redemption, that the Shekina shall return home from its exile. "That all shells may withdraw from the Shekina and that it may purify itself and unite itself with its owner in perfect unity." As a sign of this the Messiah will appear and make all beings free.

To many a Hasid it is, for the whole of his life, as if this must happen here and now. For he hears the voices of becoming roaring in the gorges and feels the seed of eternity in the ground of time as if it were in his blood. And so he can never think otherwise than that *this* moment and now *this* one will be the chosen moment. And his imagination compels him ever more fervently, for ever more commandingly speaks the voice and ever more demandingly swells the seed.

It is told of one zaddik that he awaited redemption with such eagerness that when he heard a tumult in the street, he was at once moved to ask what it was and whether the messenger had not come; and each time that he went to sleep he commanded his servant to awaken him at the very moment when the messenger came. "For the coming of the redeemer was so deeply implanted in his heart that it was as when a father awaits his only son from a distant land and stands on the watch-tower with longing in his eyes and peers through all the windows, and when one opens the door, hurries out to see whether his son has not come." Others, however, are aware of the progress of the stride, see the place and hour of the path and know the distance of the Coming One. Each thing shows them the uncompleted state of the world, the need of existence speaks to them, and the breath of the winds bears bitterness to them. The world in their eyes is like an unripe fruit. Inwardly they partake in the glory— then they look outward: all lies in battle.

When the great zaddik Rabbi Menahem was in Jerusalem, it happened that a foolish man climbed the Mount of Olives and blew the shofar trumpet. No one had seen him. A rumour spread among the people that this was the shofar blast which announced the redemption. When this came to the ears of the rabbi, he opened a window and looked out into the air of the world. And he said at once, "Here is no renewal."

This is the way of redemption: that all souls and all sparks of souls which have sprung from the primeval soul and have sunk and become scattered in all creatures at the time of the original darkening of the world or through the guilt of the ages should conclude their wandering and return home purified. The Hasidim speak of this in the parable of the prince who allows the meal to begin only when the last of the guests has entered.

All men are the abode of wandering souls. These dwell in many creatures and strive from form to form toward perfection. But those which are not able to purify themselves are caught in the "world of confusion" and make their homes in lakes of water, in stones, in plants, in animals, awaiting the redeeming hour.

It is not only souls that are everywhere imprisoned but also sparks of souls. No thing is without them. They live in all that is. Each form is their prison.

And this is the meaning and mission of kavana: that it is given to men to lift up the fallen and to free the imprisoned. Not only to wait, not only to watch for the Coming One: man can work toward the redemption of the world.

Just that is kavana: the mystery of the soul that is directed to redeem the world.

It is told of some holy men that they imagined that they might bring about redemption by storm and force. In this world—when they were so afire with the grace of ecstasy that to them, who had even embraced God, nothing appeared unattainable any longer. Or in the coming world—a dying zaddik said, "My friends have gone hence, intending to bring the Messiah, and have forgotten to do so in their rapture. But I shall not forget."

In reality, however, each can only be effective in his domain. Each man has a sphere of being in space and time which is allotted to him to be redeemed through him. Places which are heavy with unraised sparks and in which souls are fettered wait for the man who will come to them with the word of freedom. When a Hasid cannot pray in one place and goes to another, then the first place demands of him, "Why would you not speak the holy words over me? And if there is evil in me, then it is for you to redeem me." But also all journeys have secret destinations of which the traveller is unaware.

It was said of some zaddikim that they had a helping power over the wandering souls. At all times, but especially when they stood in prayer, the wanderers of eternity appeared imploring before them, wishing to receive salvation from their hands. But they also knew how to find the voiceless among the banished in the exile of a tired body or in the darkness of the elements and to upraise them.

This help is an awesome venture, set down in the midst of threatening dangers, which only the holy man can enter upon without going under. "He who has a soul may let himself down into the chasm, bound fast to the rim above through his thoughts, as through a strong rope, and will return. But he who only has life or only life and spirit, he who has not yet attained the rung of thought, for him the bond will not hold and he will fall into the depths."

But if it is only those blessed ones who can plunge tranquilly into the darkness in order to aid a soul which is abandoned to the whirlpool of wandering, it is not denied to even the least of persons to raise the lost sparks from their imprisonment and send them home.

The sparks are to be found everywhere. They are suspended in things as in sealed-off springs; they stoop in the creatures as in walled-up caves; they inhale darkness and they exhale dread; they wait. And those that dwell in space flit hither and thither around the movements of the world like light-mad butterflies, looking to see which of them they might enter in order to be redeemed through them. They all wait expectantly for freedom.

"The spark in a stone or a plant or another creature is like a complete figure which sits in the middle of the thing as in a block, so that its hands and feet cannot stretch themselves and the head lies on the knees. He who is able to lift the holy spark leads this figure into freedom, and no setting free of captives is greater than this. It is as when a king's son is rescued from captivity and brought to his father."

But the liberation does not take place through formulae of exorcism or through any kind of prescribed and special action. All this grows out of the ground of otherness, which is not the ground of kavana. No leap from the everyday into the miraculous is required. "With every action man can work on the figure of the Shekina that it may step forth out of its concealment."

It is not the matter of the action, but only its dedication that is decisive. Just that which you do in the uniformity of recurrence or in the disposition of events, just this answer of the acting person to the manifold demands of the hour, an answer acquired through practice or won through inspiration, just this continuity of the living stream leads—when accomplished in dedication—to redemption. He who prays and sings in holiness, eats and speaks in holiness, in holiness takes the prescribed ritual bath and in holiness is mindful of his business, through him the fallen sparks are raised and the fallen worlds redeemed and renewed.

Around each man—enclosed within the wide sphere of his activity— is laid a natural circle of things which, before all, he is called to set free. These are the creatures and objects that are spoken of as the possessions of this individual: his animals and his walls, his garden and his meadow, his tools and his food. In so far as he cultivates and enjoys them in holiness, he frees their souls. "For this reason a man must always be compassionate toward his tools and all his possessions."

But also in the soul itself there appear those that need liberation. Most of these are sparks which have fallen through the guilt of this soul in one of its earlier lives. They are the alien, disturbing thoughts that often come to man in prayer. "When man stands in prayer and desires to join himself to Eternity, and the alien thoughts come and descend on him, these are holy sparks that have sunken and that wish to be raised and redeemed by him; and the sparks belong to him, they are kindred to the roots of his soul: it is his own powers that he must redeem." He redeems them when he restores each troubled thought to its pure source, allows each impulse intent on a particular thing to flow into the divine creative impulse, allows everything alien to be submerged in the inalienable divine.

This is the kavana of receiving: that one redeem the sparks in the surrounding things and the sparks that draw near out of the invisible. But there is yet another kavana, the kavana of giving. It bears no stray soul-rays in helpful hands; it binds worlds to one another and rules over the mysteries, it pours itself into the thirsty distance, it gives itself to infinity. But it too has no need of miraculous deeds. Its path is creation, and the word before all other forms of creation.

From time immemorial speech was for the Jewish mystic a rare and awe-inspiring thing. A characteristic theory of letters existed which dealt with them as with the elements of the world and with their intermixture as with the inwardness of reality. The word is an abyss through which the speaker strides. "One should speak words as if the heavens were opened in them. And as if it were not so that you take the word in your mouth, but rather as if you entered into the word." He who knows the secret melody that bears the inner into the outer, who knows the holy song that merges the lonely, shy letters into the singing of the spheres, he is full of the power of God, "and it is as if he created heaven and earth and all worlds anew." He does not find his sphere before him as does the freer of souls, he extends it from the firmament to the silent depths. But he also works toward redemption. "For in each sign are the three: world, soul, and divinity. They rise and join and unite themselves, and they become the word, and the words unite themselves in God in genuine unity, since a man has set his soul in them, and worlds unite themselves and ascend, and the great rapture is born." Thus the acting person prepares the final oneness of all things.

And as avoda flowed into hitlahavut, the basic principle of Hasidic life, so there too kavana flows into hitlahavut. For creating means to be created: the divine moves and overcomes us. And to be created is ecstasy: only he who sinks into the Nothing of the Unconditioned receives the forming hand of the spirit. This is portrayed in parable. It is not given to anything in the world to be reborn and to attain to a new form unless it comes first to the Nothing, that is to the "form of the in between." No creature can exist in it, it is the power before creation and is called chaos. Thus the perishing of the egg into the chick and thus the seed, which does not sprout before it has gone down into the earth and decayed. "And this is called wisdom, that is, a thought without revelation. And so it is: if man desires that a new creation come out of him, then he must come with all his potentiality to the state of nothing, and then God brings forth in him a new creation, and he is like a fountain that does not run dry and a stream that does not become exhausted."

Thus the will of the Hasidic teaching of kavana is two-fold: that enjoyment, the internalizing of that which is without, should take place in holiness and that creation, the externalizing of that which is within, should take place in holiness. Through holy creation and through holy enjoyment the redemption of the world is accomplished.

Shiflut: Humility

God never does the same thing twice, said Rabbi Nachman of Bratzlav.

That which exists is unique, and it happens but once. New and without a past, it emerges from the flood of returnings, takes place, and plunges back into it, unrepeatable. Each thing reappears at another time, but each transformed. And the throws and falls that rule over the great world-creations, and the water and fire which shape the form of the earth, and the mixings and unmixings which brew the life of the living, and the spirit of man with all its trial-and-error relation to the yielding abundance of the possible—all of these together cannot create an identical thing nor bring back one of the things that have been sealed as belonging to the past. It is because things happen but once that the individual partakes in eternity. For the individual with his inextinguishable uniqueness is engraved in the heart of the all and lies for ever in the lap of the timeless as he who is constituted thus and not otherwise.

Uniqueness is the essential good of man that is given to him to unfold. And just this is the meaning of the return, that his uniqueness may become ever purer and more complete; and that in each new life the one who has returned may stand in ever more untroubled and undisturbed incomparability. For pure uniqueness and pure perfection are one, and he who has become so entirely individual that no otherness any longer has power over him or place in him has completed the journey and is redeemed and rests in God.

"Every man shall know and consider that in his qualities he is unique in the world and that none like him ever lived, for had there ever before been some one like him, then he would not have needed to exist. But each is in truth a new thing in the world, and he shall make perfect his special quality, for it is because it is not perfect that the coming of the Messiah tarries."

Only in his own way and not in any other can the one who strives perfect himself. "He who lays hold of the rung of his companion and lets go of his own rung, through him neither the one nor the other will be realized. Many acted like Rabbi Simeon ben Yohai and

219

in their hands it did not turn out well, for they were not of the same nature as he but only acted as they saw him act out of his nature."

But as man seeks God in lonely fervour and yet there is a high service that only the community can fulfil, and as man accomplishes enormous things with his everyday actions, yet does not do so alone but needs for such action the world and the things in it, so the uniqueness of man proves itself in his life with others. For the more unique a man really is, so much the more can he give to the other and so much the more will he give him. And this is his one sorrow, that his giving is limited by the one who takes. For "the bestower is on the side of mercy and the receiver is on the side of rigour. And so it is with each thing. As when one pours out of a large vessel into a goblet: the vessel pours from out of its fullness, but the goblet limits the gift."

The individual sees God and embraces Him. The individual redeems the fallen worlds. And yet the individual is not a whole, but a part. And the purer and more perfect he is, so much the more intimately does he know that he is a part and so much the more actively there stirs in him the community of existence. That is the mystery of humility.

"Every man has a light over him, and when the souls of two men meet, the two lights join each other and from them there goes forth one light. And this is called generation." To feel the universal generation as a sea and oneself as a wave, that is the mystery of humility.

But it is not humility when one "lowers himself too much and forgets that man can bring down an overflowing blessing on all the world through his words and his actions." This is called impure humility. "The greatest evil is when you forget that you are the son of a king." He is truly humble who feels the other as himself and himself in the other.

Haughtiness means to contrast oneself with others. The haughty man is not he who knows himself, but he who compares himself with others. No man can presume too much if he stands on his own ground since all the heavens are open to him and all the worlds devoted to him. The man who presumes too much is the man who contrasts himself with others, who sees himself as higher than the humblest of things, who rules with measure and weights and pronounces judgement.

"If Messiah should come today," a zaddik said, "and say, 'You are better than the others,' then I would say to him, 'You are not Messiah.' "

The soul of the haughty lives without product and essence; it flutters and toils and is not blessed. The thoughts whose real intent is not what is thought but themselves and their brilliance are shadows. The deed which has in mind not the goal but dominance has no body, only surface, no existence, only appearance. He who measures and weighs becomes empty and unreal like measure and weight. "In him who is full of himself there is no room for God."

It is told of one disciple that he went into seclusion and cut himself off from the things of the world in order to cling solely to the teaching and the service, and he sat alone fasting from Sabbath to Sabbath and learning and praying. But his mind, beyond all conscious purpose, was filled with pride in his action; it shone before his eyes and his fingers burned to lay it on his forehead like the diadem of the anointed. And so all his work fell to the lot of the "other side," and the divine had no share in it. But his heart drove him ever more strongly so that he did not perceive his sinking while the demons already played with his acts, and he imagined himself wholly possessed by God. Then it happened once that he leaned outside of himself and became aware of the mute and alienated things around him: Then understanding gripped him and he beheld his deeds piled up at the feet of a gigantic idol, and he beheld himself in the reeling emptiness, abandoned to the nameless. This much is told and nothing more.

But the humble man has the "drawing power." As long as a man sees himself above and before others, he has a limit, "and God cannot pour His holiness into him, for God is without limit." But when a man rests in himself as in the nothing, he is not limited by any other thing, he is limitless and God pours His glory into him.

The humility which is meant here is no willed and practised virtue. It is nothing but an inner being, feeling, and expressing. Nowhere in it is there a compulsion, nowhere a self-humbling, a self-restraining, a self-resolve. It is indivisible as the glance of a child and simple as a child's speech.

The humble man lives in each being and knows each being's manner and virtue. Since no one is to him "the other," he knows from within that none lacks some hidden value; knows that there "is no man who does not have his hour." For him, the colours of the world do not blend with one another, rather each soul stands before him in the majesty of its particular existence. "In each man there is a priceless treasure that is in no other. Therefore, one shall honour each man for the hidden value that only he and none of his comrades has."

"God does not look on the evil side," said one zaddik; "how should I dare to do so?"

He who lives in others according to the mystery of humility can condemn no one. "He who passes sentence on a man has passed it on himself."

He who separates himself from the sinner departs in guilt. But the saint can suffer for the sins of a man as for his own. Only living with the other is justice.

Living with the other as a form of knowing is justice. Living with the other as a form of being is love. For that feeling that is called love among men, the feeling of being near and of wishing to be near a few, is nothing other than a recollection from a heavenly life: "Those who sat next to one another in Paradise and were neighbours and relatives, they are also near to one another in this world." But in truth love is all-comprehensive and sustaining and is extended to all the living without selection and distinction. "How can you say of me that I am a leader of the generation," said a zaddik, "when I still feel in myself a stronger love for those near me and for my seed than for all men?" That this attitude also extends to animals is shown by the accounts of Rabbi Wolf who could never shout at a horse, of Rabbi Moshe Leib, who gave drink to the neglected calves at the market, of Rabbi Susya who could not see a cage, "and the wretchedness of the bird and its anxiety to fly in the air of the world and to be a free wanderer in accordance with its nature," without opening it. But it is not only the beings to whom the short-sighted gaze of the crowd accords the name of "living" who are embraced by the love of the loving man: "There is no thing in the world in which there is not life, and each has received from his life the form in which it stands before your eyes. And lo, this life is the life of God."

Thus it is held that the love of the living is love of God, and it is higher than any other service. A master asked one of his disciples, "You know that two forces cannot occupy the human mind at the same time. If then you rise from your couch to-morrow and two ways are before you: the love of God and the love of man, which should come first?" "I do not know," the latter answered. Then spoke the master, "It is written in the prayer-book that is in the hands of the people, 'Before you pray, say the words, Love thy companion as one like thyself.' Do you think that the venerable ones commanded that without purpose? If some one says to you that he has love for God but has no love for the living, he speaks falsely and pretends that which is impossible."

Therefore, when one has departed from God, the love of a man is his only salvation. When a father complained to the Baal-Shem, "My son is estranged from God—what shall I do?" he replied, "Love him more."

This is one of the primary Hasidic words: to love more. Its roots sink deep and stretch out far. He who has understood this can learn to understand Judaism anew. There is a great moving force therein.

A great moving force and yet again only a lost sound. It is a lost sound, when somewhere—in that dark windowless room—and at some time—in those days without the power of message—the lips of a nameless, soon-to-be-forgotten man, of the zaddik Rabbi Rafael, form these words, "If a man sees that his companion hates him, he shall love him the more. For the community of the living is the carriage of God's majesty, and where there is a rent in the carriage, one must fill it, and where there is so little love that the joining comes apart, one must love more on one's own side to overcome the lack."

Once before a journey this Rabbi Rafael called to a disciple that he should sit beside him in the carriage. "I fear I shall make it too crowded for you," the latter responded. But the rabbi now spoke in an exalted voice, "So we shall love each other more: then there will be room enough for us."

They may stand here as a witness, the symbol and the reality, separate and yet one and inseparable, the carriage of the Shekina and the carriage of the friends.

trusted friends. He has no fear of the before and the after, of the above and the below, of this world and the world to come. He is at home and never can be cast out. The earth cannot help but be his cradle, and heaven cannot help but be his mirror and his echo.

APPENDIX C:– THE *HUI MING CHING.*

The *Hui Ming Ching* is a Taoist scripture written in 1794 by Liu Hua-yang. Many Buddhist writers have decried this work because of its emphasis on undertaking meditation for worldly longevity and physical well-being as the only worthwhile goals of life. It is presented here for purposes of comparison both with the plates of this book and with "The Life of the Hasidim." The reader should take care to remember that there are substantial differences in the Buddhist, Judaic, and Taoist traditions and should not get caught in the obvious limitations of the *Hui Ming Ching* (i.e. longevity and worldly gain).

The text presented here is from *The Secret of the Golden Flower*, translated from the Chinese by Richard Wilhelm and from Wilhelm's German translation by Cary F. Baynes, published by Harcourt Brace Jovanovich, Inc., New York, 1962. The illustrations have been re-drawn for this publication, as the detail in the originals is frequently difficult to discern. The poems and captions for the pictures are our own translations from the original Chinese. Our translations are temporary ones, and several words had to be deleted due to the poor quality of the reproduction of the original Chinese, which rendered several characters illegible. A complete translation of these poems and a retranslation of the text should appear in the next edition.

Daizui MacPhillamy

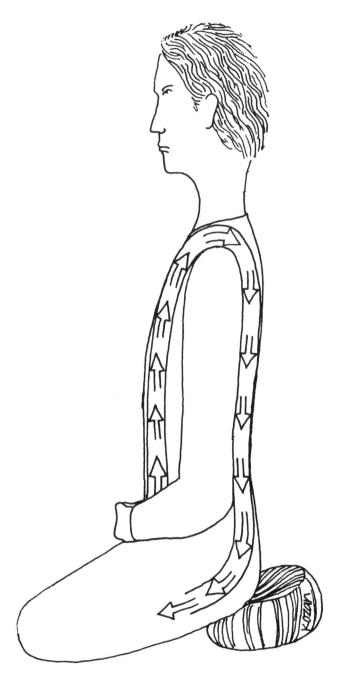

Fig. 1.

Fig. 2. The Chart of Zazen. Meditation, Stage 1.

Sitting for a long time, forgetting knowledge, one
    suddenly realises the moon in the earth.
Quietly the heavenly wind comes leaping to arrive at
    the liver and lungs.
He looks down at one deep pool of perfectly clear
    water with not a thing out of place.
In the middle the weaving - - - roams silently in perfect
    accord with itself.

Without external matters one day is like two days in
    this quiet sitting.
So, if one lives for seventy years, it is just as if one
    lived for a hundred and forty.
Sitting quietly, with few thoughts and few desires,
The Lord of the House nourishes the essence and
    preserves the spirit (mind).

I. CESSATION OF OUTFLOWING

If thou wouldst complete the diamond body with
no outflowing,
Diligently heat the roots of consciousness and life.
Kindle light in the blessed country ever close at
hand,
And there hidden, let thy true self always dwell.

(The illustration found here in the Chinese text shows
the body of a man. In the middle of the lower half of
the body is drawn a germ cell by which the gateway of
life is separated from the gateway of consciousness. In
between, leading to the outside world, is the canal
through which the vital fluids flow out.[1] See Fig. 1.)

The subtlest secret of the Tao is human nature
and life (*hsing-ming*). There is no better way of culti-
vating human nature and life than to bring both back
to unity. The holy men of ancient times, and the great
sages, set forth their thoughts about the unification of
human nature and life by means of images from the
external world; they were reluctant to speak of it openly without allegories. Therefore the secret of how to
cultivate both simultaneously was lost on earth. What I
show through a series of images is not a frivolous giving
away of secrets. On the contrary, because I combined
the notes of the *Leng-yen-ching* on the cessation of
outflowing and the secret thoughts of *Hua-yen-ching*
with occasional references to the other sutras, in order

---

1. This explanatory note and those that follow were
contributed by Richard Wilhelm. (C. F. B.) [Those
marked (H. W.) were furnished by Hellmut Wilhelm.]

to summarize them in this true picture, it can be understood that consciousness and life are not anything external to the germinal vesicle. I have drawn this picture so that companions pursuing the divine workings of the dual cultivation may know that in this way the true seed matures, that in this way the cessation of outflowing is brought about, that in this way the *sheli*[2] is melted out, that in this way the great Tao is completed.

But the germinal vesicle is an invisible cavern; it has neither form nor image. When the vital breath stirs, the seed of this vesicle comes into being; when it ceases it disappears again. It is the place which harbours truth, the altar upon which consciousness and life are made. It is called the dragon castle at the bottom of the sea, the boundary region of the snow mountains, the primordial pass, the kingdom of greatest joy, the boundless country. All these different names mean this germinal vesicle. If a dying man does not know this germinal vesicle, he will not find the unity of consciousness and life in a thousand births, nor in ten thousand aeons.

This germinal point is something great. Before this our body is born of our parents, at the time of conception, this seed is first created and human nature and life dwell therein. The two are intermingled and form a unity, inseparably mixed like the sparks in the refining furnace, a combination of primordial harmony and divine law. Therefore it is said: 'In the state before the appearance there is an inexhaustible breath.' Furthermore it is said: 'Before the parents have begotten the child, the breath of life is complete and the embryo perfect.' But when the embryo moves and the embryo vesicle is torn, it is as if a man lost his footing on a high

---

2. *Sarira*, the firm, that is the immortal body.

mountain: with a cry the man plunges down to earth, and from then on human nature and life are divided. From this moment human nature can no longer see life nor life human nature. And now fate takes its course: youth passes over into maturity, maturity into old age, and old age into woe.

Therefore the Julai,[3] in his great compassion, let the secret making and melting be made known. He teaches one to re-enter the womb and create anew the human nature and life of the ego; he shows how spirit and soul (vital breath) enter the germinal vesicle, how they must combine to become a unity in order to complete the true fruit, just as the sperm[4] and soul of father and mother entered this germinal vesicle and united as one being in order to complete the embryo. The principle is the same.

Within the germinal vesicle is the fire of the ruler; at the entrance of the germinal vesicle is the fire of the minister; in the whole body, the fire of the people. When the fire of the ruler expresses itself, it is received by the fire of the minister. When the fire of the minister moves, the fire of the people follows him. When the three fires express themselves in this order a man develops. But when the three fires return in reverse order the Tao develops.

This is the reason that all the sages began their work at the germinal vesicle in which outflowing had ceased. If one does not establish this path, but sets up other things, it is of no avail. Therefore all the schools and sects which do not know that the ruling principle of consciousness and life is in this germinal vesicle, and which therefore seek it in the outer world, can accomplish nothing despite all their efforts to find it outside.

---

3. The Buddha Tathagata.

4. *Ching*, the sperm, is the masculine element; *ch'i*, soul, breath-energy, is the feminine, receptive element.

2. THE SIX PERIODS OF CIRCULATION IN CONFORMITY WITH THE LAW[5]

If one discerns the beginning of the Buddha's path,
There will be the blessed city of the West.
After the circulation in conformity with the law,
    there is a turn upward towards heaven when the
    breath is drawn in.
When the breath flows out energy is directed
    towards the earth.
One time-period consists of six intervals (*hou*).
In two intervals one gathers Moni (Sakyamuni).
The great Tao comes forth from the centre.
Do not seek the primordial seed outside!

The most marvellous effect of the Tao is the circulation in conformity with the law. What makes the movement inexhaustible is the path. What best regulates the speed are the rhythms (*kuei*). What best determines the number of the exercises is the method of the intervals (*hou*).

This presentation contains the whole law, and the true features of the Buddha from the West are contained in it. The secrets contained in it show how one gets control of the process by exhaling and inhaling, how the alternation between decrease and increase expresses itself in closing and opening, how one needs true thoughts in order not to deviate from the way, how the firm delimitation of the regions makes it possible to begin and to stop at the right time.

---

5. This concept has been borrowed from Buddhist terminology, in the context of which it is usually translated as the 'Wheel of the Law'. (H. W.)

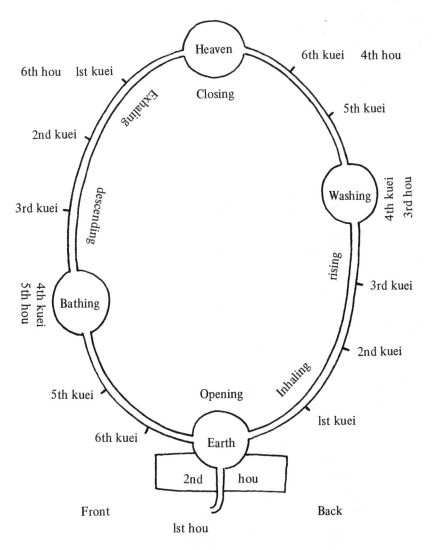

Fig. 3. The Six Periods of Circulation in Conformity
with the Law.

I sacrifice myself and serve man, because I have presented fully this picture which reveals the heavenly seed completely, so that every layman and man of the world can reach it and so bring it to completion. He who lacks the right virtue may well find something in it, but heaven will not grant him his Tao. Why not? The right virtue belongs to the Tao as does one wing of a bird to the other: if one is lacking, the other is of no use. Therefore there is needed loyalty and reverence, humaneness and justice and strict adherence to the five commandments[6]; then only does one have the prospect of attaining something.

But all the subtleties and secrets are offered in this *Book of Consciousness and Life* to be pondered and weighed, so that one can attain everything in its truth.

(The drawing is intended to show the circulation of the streams of energy during the movement of breathing. Inhalation is accompanied by the sinking of the abdomen and exhalation by the lifting of it, but in these exercises the point is that we have a backward-flowing movement as follows: when inhaling, one opens the lower energy-gate and allows the energy to rise upward along the rear line of energy [in the spinal cord] , and this upward flow corresponds to the time-intervals indicated in the drawing. In exhaling, the upper gate is closed and the stream of energy is allowed to flow downward along the front line, likewise in the order of the time-intervals indicated. Furthermore, it is to be noted that the stations for 'washing' and 'bathing' do not lie exactly in the middle of the lines, but that 'washing' is somewhat above and 'bathing' somewhat below the middle, as the drawing shows. See Fig. 3.)

6. The Buddhist five commandments are: (l) not to kill; (2) not to steal; (3) not to commit adultery; (4) not to lie; (5) not to drink and not to eat meat.

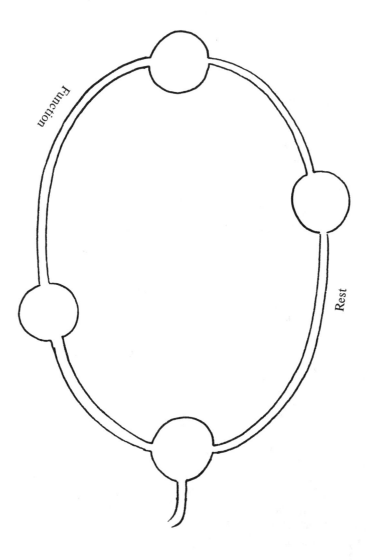

Fig. 4. The Two Energy-Paths of Function and Rest.

3. THE TWO ENERGY-PATHS
OF FUNCTION AND CONTROL

There appears the way of the in-breathing and out-breathing of the primordial pass.
Do not forget the white path below the circulation in conformity with the law!
Always let the cave of eternal life be nourished through the fire!
Ah! Test the immortal place of the gleaming pearl!

(In the text there is another picture here which is very similar to the first. It shows again the paths of energy: the one in front leads down and is called the function-path [*jen*], and the one at the back leading upwards is the control-path [*tu*]. See Fig. 4.)

This picture is really the same as the one that precedes it. The reason that I show it again is so that the person striving for cultivation of the Tao may know that there is in his own body a circulation in conformity with the law. I have furnished this picture in order to enlighten companions in search of the goal. When these two paths (the functioning and the controlling) can be brought into unbroken connection, then all energy-paths are joined. The deer sleeps with his nose on his tail in order to close his controlling energy-path. The crane and the tortoise close their functioning-paths. Hence these three animals become at least a thousand years old. How much further can a man go! A man who carries on the cultivation of the Tao, who sets in motion the circulation in conformity with the law, in order to let consciousness and life circulate, need not fear that he is not lengthening his life and is not completing his path.

Fig. 5. The Chart of the Appearance of the Son of the Lord. Meditation, Stage 2.

1. Now spirituality ripens; the compassionate mother certainly cherishes the child.

   The arrangement of the spaces between inhalation and exhalation of the breath is called the limitless treasury.

   The treasury enfolded in the hara enfolds emptiness.

   I ask, "Within emptiness who is the believer?" He replies, "Your Eternal Lord."

2. Walking, standing, sitting, lying, cherishing the body, protecting the mind (spirit),

   In this way Real Life is preserved endlessly thinking from the centre of your being.

3. To be a husband is like being a wasp or insect.

   The offspring of pregnant mosquitos pass on their affections and are mutually friendly.

   Their essence harmonises their spirits;

   Following this way all things, great and small, reach their reality.

4. He flies above the sun and the clouds to see the Real Man in the Imperial Court.

   The hidden dragon is now transformed into a flying dragon.

   IT - - - appears, the Spirit passes freely and cannot be deprived.

   One sunrise *IT* jumps out beyond the radiance of the jewel and,

   Producing the Son of the Lord, arrives straightway at the Heavenly Court.

5. The water of the Spirit flows full and gently forth,
   Deeply flooding the root and the trunk;
   Within and without nothing is produced
   Thus nourishing long the sage's deepset eyes.

4. THE EMBRYO OF THE TAO

According to the law, but without exertion, one
must diligently fill oneself with light.
Forgetting appearance, look within and help the
true spiritual power!
Ten months the embryo is under fire.
After a year the washings and baths become warm.

(The picture that belongs here corresponds to the one
shown as Fig. 5.)

This picture will be found in the original edition
of the *Leng-yen-ching*. But the ignorant monks who
did not recognize the hidden meaning and knew nothing
about the embryo of the Tao have for this reason made
the mistake of leaving this picture out. I only found
out through the explanations of adepts that the Julai
(Tathagata) knows real work on the embryo of the Tao.
This embryo is nothing corporeally visible which might
be completed by other beings, but is in reality the spiritual breath-energy of the ego. First the spirit must
penetrate the breath-energy (the soul), then the breath-
energy envelops the spirit. When spirit and breath-energy
are firmly united and the thoughts quiet and immobile,
this is described as the embryo. The breath-energy must
crystallize; only then will the spirit become effective.
Therefore it is said in the *Leng-yen-ching*: 'Take mater-
nal care of the awakening and the answering.' The two
energies nourish and strengthen one another. Therefore
it is said: 'Daily growth takes place.' When the energy
is strong enough and the embryo is round and complete
it comes out of the top of the head. This is what is
called: the completed appearance which comes forth as
embryo and begets itself as the son of the Buddha.

5. THE BIRTH OF THE FRUIT

Outside the body there is a body called the Buddha
image.
The thought which is powerful, the absence of
thoughts, is Bodhi.
The thousand-petalled lotus flower opens, transformed through breath-energy.
Because of the crystallization of the spirit, a hundredfold splendour shines forth.

(The picture that belongs here corresponds to the one
shown as Fig. 6.)

In the *Leng-yen-chou*[7] it is said: 'At that time
the ruler of the world caused a hundredfold precious
light to beam from his hair knots. In the midst of the
light shone the thousand-petalled, precious lotus flower.
And there within the flower sat a transformed Julai.
And from the top of his head went ten rays of white,
precious light, which were visible everywhere. The
crowd looked up to the out-streaming light and the
Julai announced: "The divine, magic mantra is the appearance of the light-spirit, therefore his name is Son
of Buddha." '

If a man does not receive the teaching about consciousness and life, but merely repeats meditation formulae stolidly and in solitude, how could there develop
out of his own body the Julai, who sits and shines
forth in the lotus flower and appears in his own spirit-
body! Many say that the light-spirit is a minor teaching;
but how can that which a man receives from the ruler

---

7. *Suramgama* mantra. (H. W.)

of the world be a minor teaching? Herewith I have betrayed the deepest secret of the *Leng-yen* in order to teach disciples. He who receives this way rises at once to the dark secret and no longer becomes submerged in the dust of everyday life.

Fig. 6. The Chart of the Setting Up of the Pillar of the Lord of the House. Meditation, Stage 3.

Not yet having arrived at the other shore he cannot do without things.
On arriving at the other shore things can be used again;
In the middle of the forehead there is a constant point of white light;
And, instead of doing it themselves, fools wait to ask a Bodhisattva!

The First Prince erects the pillar and sits in the mysterious city;
Three white cranes dance with eight mates.
Changing pure - - - causes the harmony of heaven and earth;
Eternal life causes this - - - time.

Passing the light outside he houses the Spirit within.
The Lord of the House arrives quickly and joins the auspicious association.
With no mind in affairs he has no affairs in mind;
Leaping out of the myriad illusions, - - - one cloud.

Fig. 7. The Retention of the Transformed Body.
Meditation, Stage 4.

6. CONCERNING THE RETENTION OF THE TRANSFORMED BODY

Every separate thought takes shape and becomes
visible in colour and form.

The total spiritual power unfolds its traces and
transforms itself into emptiness.

Going out into being and going into non-being, one
completes the miraculous Tao.

All separate shapes appear as bodies, united with a
true source.

(The picture that belongs here corresponds to the one
shown as Fig. 7.)

7. THE FACE TURNED TO THE WALL

The shapes formed by the spirit-fire are only empty
colours and forms.
The light of human nature [*hsing*] shines back on
the primordial, the true.
The imprint of the heart floats in space; untarnished,
the moonlight shines.
The boat of life has reached the shore; bright shines
the sunlight.

(The picture that belongs here corresponds to the one
shown as Fig. 2.)

8. EMPTY INFINITY

Without beginning, without end,
Without past, without future.
A halo of light surrounds the world of the law.
We forget one another, quiet and pure, altogether
    powerful and empty.
The emptiness is irradiated by the light of the heart
    and of heaven.
The water of the sea is smooth and mirrors the moon
    in its surface.
The clouds disappear in blue space; the mountains
    shine clear.
Consciousness reverts to contemplation; the moon-
    disk rests alone.

(The picture that belongs here is the one shown as
Fig. 8.)

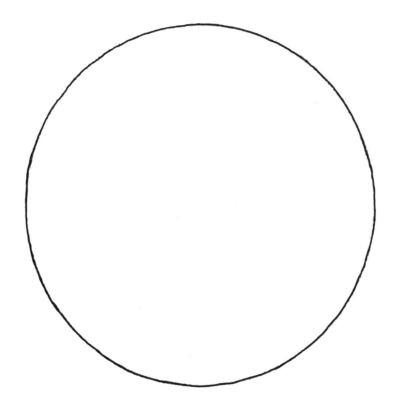

Fig. 8.

APPENDIX D:– QUESTIONS AND ANSWERS.

The following questions and answers were recorded during discussions of both monks and lay Buddhists with Kennett Rōshi on the subject of this book. They have been edited, paraphrased, and printed here in hopes that they may clarify some of the questions which readers may have.

QUESTION: Suppose I experience visions or other things, how can I tell if they are really religious experiences, or if I'm going crazy, or if they are makyo–delusions and illusions that arise either from the selfish mind or simply from an incorrect meditation posture?

Kennett Rōshi: Experiences are experiences; they don't *mean* anything.

Monk: But suppose I do start seeing things, what do I do?

Kennett Rōshi: That's up to you; you are not me. I know what I did, I just sat still and watched them. I did Zazen and continued my training.

Second Monk: Just do your training, do your meditation. Kenshōs take care of themselves. For goodness sake don't think, "Oooh–something's going to happen!" every time something a little unusual comes up in your meditation. You can waste years doing that.

Third Monk: And what if someone comes to you and says he's been seeing lotus blossoms?

251

Kennett Rōshi: If someone says he sees lotus blossoms and towers, I shall say, "Is that so?" and if he says, "I'm seeing devils and demons," I shall say, "Is that so?" He has to decide what he will do. I have told you what I did. Yes, I saw lotus blossoms and towers; I saw Buddhas; I saw Patriarchs: I loved and enjoyed it. And here I am still sitting here with a bunch of monks.

QUESTION: Do you have any theories about why this happened to you at the present time; was there anything special about you that made Heaven choose you for this experience?

Kennett Rōshi: We choose Heaven; Heaven does not choose us. When we are willing to pay the price that the Lord of the House demands for entrance, the gateless gate opens automatically. There is nothing special about me; I am neither holy nor unholy, enlightened nor unenlightened. I was born Peg Kennett and I will die Peg Kennett.

Monk: Many people look for a saint who can do the work for them.

Kennett Rōshi: There's a passage of the *Hui Ming Ching* which says, "And the fools wait to ask a Bodhisattva." You can do it yourself, and the fools wait to ask a Bodhisattva. You have to deal with your karma; there is no saviour who can take it away.

QUESTION: I have heard it said that some schools of Buddhism maintain that women cannot have this sort of understanding. How do you explain this?

Kennett Rōshi: Zen has always recognized the fact that a woman can have full kenshō experience. The opinions you speak of are peculiar to schools of

Buddhism that have not tended to move with the times, preferring to retain the ancient social opinions of women prevalent in the area from which the school originated, which has led them to tend to stifle or at least keep silent about the spiritual ability of women.

QUESTION: What do you mean when you say that nothing matters? It sounds so negative.

Kennett Rōshi: There is *no thing* that matters; neither life nor death, good nor bad, form nor void—no opposites matter at all. Be in the mind of Zazen constantly; trust in the Lord of the House completely; follow the voice in your heart; be willing to accept everything and give up everything; and at the same time know your complete responsibility for all you do. Do not grab onto anything. It is actually very positive—go on with the flow of life.

Lay Buddhist: In a sense, then, nothing matters and at the same time everything matters a great deal—in terms of being absolutely responsible for what you do.

Kennett Rōshi: Yes. A volume can be written on this question and nothing will answer it completely; you must find out for yourself.

Monk: Experiencing 'Nothing Matters' with your whole being is the same as absolute love for all beings.

QUESTION: What should I do if I start to have a kenshō experience at work or if I have one where there is no priest to talk to? I'm almost afraid to meditate hard enough in case it were to happen.

253

Kennett Rōshi: Keep your mouth shut unless you know a Zen Master or any person you can really trust who knows about this sort of thing.

Monk: There have been some awful examples of people who have had valid religious experiences and ended up in mental institutions because they confided in the wrong people.

Second Monk: Remember also that it is not the experience *per se* which is important. Not all kenshōs are accompanied by visions, and not everyone who has visions is having a kenshō. A kenshō shows you how to train better—how to straighten up your life. You don't have to have visions; and if they come, you don't have to tell anyone unless you can trust them. What is really important is to go on and straighten up your life.

Third Monk: This is why kenshōs usually do not happen unless a person has meditated and trained himself in the Precepts for some time. There is too much of a danger of getting attached to the kenshō experience and not going on with the training. In any case, the question is really whether you are going to train or not. If you are, then you don't have much choice about whether or not to meditate with all your might, regardless of the fears you may have.

QUESTION: If I experience a past life in which I murdered someone or engaged in witchcraft or the like, does that mean that I am mentally unbalanced or that I am "that kind of person" in this life?

Kennett Rōshi: No.

Monk: In fact, I know of several people who have seen such past lives. They are not doing such things now, nor are they mentally ill. They are healthy, normal, productive people. One finds out such things in order to know one's potential for creating suffering and to see better how one is creating it in this life.

Second Monk: If you cannot conceive of doing such things, if you do not know that you *could* murder, for instance, then you are not capable of fully feeling empathy and compassion for your fellow man and you have a blind spot in your training. Meditation shows you your freedom. Every one *could* commit murder; we all could do the most perverted and horrible things, and we all can be Buddha. Unless you can experience this as a real choice and make that choice fully aware of your freedom to choose and of your absolute responsibility for what you choose, you cannot know how to train fully as a spiritual adult.

QUESTION: Are the practice of Zazen and the other things you wrote about in *Zen is Eternal Life* enough, or are there new practices you advocate undertaking?

Kennett Rôshi: How do you think this happened to me? I did Zazen; I studied the Scriptures in detail; I followed the Precepts. The only "new" practice (if such it can be called) is my explicit explanation of how to follow the breath. Please don't get stuck with the experiences I describe in this book; don't get fascinated—I cannot say this too often! What is happening to you now is the very best teaching for you now—accept it, be grateful, learn from it—and do not long for other people's experiences. In other words, do your own training.

Monk: If someone comes to Shasta Abbey expecting to see people with lotus blossoms on their heads running around reliving past lives, he's going to be very disappointed! We do Zazen; we have ceremonies; we read the Scriptures; we eat, sleep, and use the toilet. Mostly we work hard.

Lay Buddhist: I wonder if these experiences could be induced artificially, say by drugs, hypnotic regression, or autosuggestion.

Monk: We haven't tried, so I don't know. There's a darned good reason we haven't, too. Kenshō, and other religious experiences, happen *naturally*, when one's training is strong enough to make good use of them. To try to force them artificially is not only to try to rob the Treasure House of your own heart but also to risk serious spiritual, mental, and physical illness.

Second Monk: It has been suggested, though, that autosuggestion might account for the experiences that some of us have had in becoming aware of past lives, even though we don't consciously try to do this. After all, at times when someone is going through this, there are several people there with him and sometimes we use a form of Oriental massage to help ease the tensions.

First Monk: As with any form of psychologism, you cannot prove this either way, of course. In my own experience, having people whom I trust and love present helped me face the kōan, and having the massage simply aided in relaxing away the tensions of my body and mind. After all, moxa burning, acupuncture, acupressure, *do-in,* and similar forms of massage have been used in Zen monasteries for centuries; we are not doing something new on that score.

Third Monk: What about asking our friend, here? As a professional psychologist, could you give an opinion? You have been with us here now for several days and have had contact with some of us for a number of years. In your professional opinion, would you say that autosuggestion, hypnotic phenomena, or some sort of hysterical behavior are going on here?

Visiting Psychologist: There is no doubt in my mind that that's not the right explanation. For example, all of you are speaking with your own voices, your own words; you are not talking like Kennett Rōshi; you are independent people who obviously have minds of your own and are not afraid to use them. Several of you have spoken of your own experiences, and they were not copies of Kennett Rōshi's experiences. If they had been, they would have been flat, two-dimensional, and useless.

Third Monk: One of the things Rōshi teaches us is to be adult, independent, and responsible for our actions. I have sometimes disagreed with what Rōshi has done and I have told her so. She is still my master and I am still her disciple. My respect and love for her continues to deepen, but we can still disagree on some things. Occasionally monks have felt that they should go away from here, and they leave. I think that this is good; it is healthy. We are certainly not a bunch of zombies or automata. For some, there is a time to stay and a time to go.

QUESTION: Does the kenshō you describe here ever happen except after long years of training and meditation?

Kennett Rōshi: Yes, the opportunity is offered to everyone at the moment of death, to each in their own way. That is why it is incredibly important to be with and love someone at that moment, and not to interfere in this process. Of course, it is better not to wait until that moment before being willing to look so closely at yourself, but most people aren't willing to risk that much until then. People who are not willing to accept absolutely, as part of their lives, the full implication of the Buddhist Precepts or Judeo-Christian Commandments, for example, in their fullest and deepest meaning, have no possibility of experiencing this kenshō in life. Absolute commitment is necessary to repentance of the past and living by the Lord's will for the future. If this kenshō is to take place before death and the person survive in life as we know it to talk about it, then no matter what his religion (or lack of religion) he must be *converted* from his former behavior and understand the Three Pure Precepts absolutely in his own tradition. For someone who has no religion, this could present a problem, although where the Lord of the House is, there will be a way. One of the real uses of religion, as I understand it, is that during the course of training you have Scriptures and Precepts that can be used as guidelines during and after this conversion. Atheists and materialists, having no Scriptures or Precepts to my knowledge that are readily available in collected works, have the added problem of working it all out from scratch at the last minute.

QUESTION: Suppose I'm in the hospital dying. The doctors want to fill me full of drugs and my family doesn't want to talk about death. Someone gives me this book. What do I do now; who do I talk to?
Kennett Rōshi: Train with all your strength; clean up your life; do not be afraid to look at everything

that comes up. Do not expect anything in particular—do not expect the same thing that happened to me. Calm your mind—be very still, very attentive, very accepting of whatever teaching the Lord of the House presents to you. It will be right for you. Know that you are not alone and know that the Lord of the House will never reject you—so do not reject Him and the opportunity and teaching that is being offered to you. *Nothing* can stop you from knowing what is in your own heart. Even if there is no one to talk to, you and the Lord of the House will do just fine.

QUESTION: Suppose I am with a friend or relative who is dying; what should I do?

Kennett Rōshi: Above all, *love them*; you must not reject them or their illness under any circumstances. Be with them and love them.

Monk: But do not cling to them; allow them to die.

Kennett Rōshi: Yes, they must be allowed to go, but there must be no rejection. Do not attempt to impose your ideas on them; do not try to convert them; do not, in other words, put yourself between them and the Lord of the House. A dying person needs to know that he is loved both by man and the Cosmic Buddha. You do your part; the Cosmic Buddha will take care of His.

QUESTION: You have said a number of things about how you will live—eating certain things, not using medications and anaesthetics, celibacy—are you suggesting that we all live this way?

Kennett Rōshi: No. I am saying that *for me*; these are things I have learned *for me*; I am not saying that anyone else should do them. You must meditate and find what is right *for you*, and it may not be the same as what is right for me. I trust my body to tell me what it needs. If it tells me that I need a medication or an anaesthetic, for instance, I will take them; if it tells me that it does not, then I won't. At present, it tells me not to do so under any circumstances. So, fine; I will not. Your body is not mine; find out for yourself what is right for you.

Visiting Psychologist: It is important that people understand that what you have written is your understanding of your own body. Most people don't have that degree of understanding of themselves and so they want to grab onto your conclusions and use them for themselves. They lose sight of the important thing—the whole process of how you came to those conclusions.

Monk: Yes, and remember that even when Rōshi makes a general statement about a thing, she is saying that one should avoid getting attached to it, not that you absolutely cannot do it. Take, for example, the statement that the type of kenshō she had requires celibacy. Rōshi is *not* saying that young people should not get married and have children.

Kennett Rōshi: Absolutely right. And on the matter of celibacy, please remember my age and yours. What I wrote was right for me at age fifty-three. Most of you are in your twenties and thirties—there is a difference, you know. Now, if you have had the first kenshōs and want the harmonisation of body and mind at your age, you are going to have to pay the price—and part of that price is dealing with sexual desire.

Monk: Even should you choose celibacy, it does not mean the repression of sexual feelings nor does it mean that orgasm may never occur. Suppose you are not married and wish to be celibate, when your body requires an orgasm it will occur spontaneously, usually when you are sleeping, and there is no need either to try to stop this or to masturbate or otherwise try to make it occur. This is another application of meditation: do not be attached and do not push away. Naturally-occurring orgasms will happen, and they do not damage one's spiritual growth.

Kennett Rōshi: This is true, and it has happened to me since this experience, and it has occurred naturally. Having had this experience has not turned me into a sort of dried prune, you know. Kenshōs make you fully alive, including sexually; they do not hinder or repress that which is normal to a live human being, and there are no attachments either of body or mind.

QUESTION: You wrote at one point of "looking in" on some of the monks who had left; is this a customary practice?

Kennett Rōshi: No, it is not. This happened naturally to show me how to use the second and third columns. This is not a practice. Don't worry, I don't read minds! Incidentally, there is a law of confidentiality in Buddhism. The following statement represents our position thereon and I follow it absolutely.

Practice of the Reformed Sōtō Zen Church
on the Confidentiality of Communications.

A priest in Buddhism is not viewed, as in
Christianity, as a mediator between man and God,
but between man and his own heart or conscience.
It must be clearly kept in mind that Zen recognises
that one cannot do evil or be irresponsible and escape the consequences simply by not recognising
an act as evil or by refusing to recognise one's
responsibility. The statements and actions of both
a priest and a penitent must be viewed in light of
this standard. A priest may not make or allow
others to make a mistake in Buddhism.

An on-going relationship between a priest and
disciple (either lay or monastic) creates a presump-
tion of confidentiality. The priest has a responsibility to the disciple to recognise his spiritual
worth, to not take over his will or lead his life for
him. The disciple has the responsibility to follow
the direction of the priest without compromising
his own conscience. Communications within these
limits are considered confidential.

In casual relationships not based on a master-
disciple relationship or in communication with
someone unfamiliar with Buddhist principles, the
priest will normally consider any penitential communication confidential provided the priest does
not allow the penitent to make a mistake in Buddhism, the confidentiality does not endanger the
life, health or safety of a third party, and the penitent is actually penitent, remorseful or contrite
and willing to accept responsibility for his actions.
A priest shall not reveal information given to him
by one who believes himself to be dying.

QUESTION: When you were having the experiences you wrote about, were you awake or in a dream state? Did you leave your body and actually go to these places or did the experiences superimpose themselves upon what you would normally see around you?

Kennett Rōshi: It superimposed itself on what was around me. I tried to close my eyes on occasion and I was absolutely forced *not* to, except on the occasions I mentioned, so that I would stay in a context that I knew. I knew that I was in the room and at the same time I was quite genuinely moving and doing things. I was aware of things going on around me, conversed with people, and did not leave my body.

QUESTION: How can I know whether I am aware of the voice of the Lord of the House or whether I am hearing my own delusions?

Monk: There are times when I *don't* know, but generally you do know. You have to trust and act accordingly; the results will show you soon enough if you were listening to the Lord or to your own selfish desires. If it was the latter, things will be in an awful mess, real soon.

Second Monk: After a while you can tell by whether or not what you hear goes against the Three Pure Precepts, but eventually you know because when it is the Lord of the House, there is a smile in your heart.

Kennett Rōshi: Yes, there's a certainty in your heart. You just have to go into it and trust that little voice. Every one of us from childhood has heard that little voice and at some time or other made a conscious decision to turn away from it. It was that moment which was the separation of body and mind, the dis-harmony, the going into duality. When you start listening to that still, small voice again, sometimes you will make mistakes, but once you really trust it, it will be the right voice.

QUESTION: In view of the reality of past lives, what do you think about spiritualism?

Kennett Rōshi: Keep away from spiritualists; however, there are spiritualists and spiritualists—it depends on what the spiritualist is doing. If he wants you to *become* your past life, to perpetuate the situation, then it is extraordinarily dangerous. If you learn something from it about yourself, the mistakes you are making or could easily make in *this* life, then it may be valuable. The grave danger of spiritualism is attachment and fascination.

Lay Buddhist: Suppose I find that I was connected with someone both in a past life and in this life—what is the appropriate attitude towards that person?

Kennett Rōshi: The first thing you have to do is *love* them. The person you are with now is *not* the person from the past life, nor are you; all you have both done is to inherit their karmic streams *in order to convert them.* Just love the other person and do not perpetuate the mistakes of the past.

Visiting Psychologist: What happens if someone comes to the Abbey and says, "I was your spiritual master in the last life. I taught you all you knew, and now I'm ready to take over the job again."

Kennett Rōshi: My answer is, "And that was a past life; this is a new life—it no longer applies. Go learn from it yourself; see the impregnations in this life of your past karma, learn from it, and convert it.

Goodbye." And if he does not say, "Goodbye," we'll call the Sheriff. After all, I know who my master in past lives was.

QUESTION: There is another way people can grossly misinterpret this book, and that is psychologism. The reaction would be something like this: everything that you experienced was the product of what was going on in your psyche at the time; it was symbols produced by your own desires, memories, and the like.

Monk: I see no way of proving this scientifically one way or the other. From the point of view of religious training, however, it makes a great deal of difference when this sort of experience happens to you. Do you set yourself apart from and above it, analyze it in terms of psychological processes and symbols, and render it one more "interesting experience," or do you open yourself to it completely, bow in gratitude, allow it to become part of yourself, and thus learn from it how to live a better life? It is vitally important neither to be attached to such experiences (the mistake of spiritualism) nor to push them away (the mistake of psychologism). Neither mess around trying to make them happen nor try to cut them off or rationalize them into a comfortable form.

Kennett Rōshi: When these things happen they happen, that's all. I do not know how, but I know why: they happen when you are ready to understand your kōan. Therefore what you must do is meditate and do not get involved in thoughts when they are going on.

Visiting Psychologist: What I think you are doing is making real a dimension of religion that has so

265

often been cut out by the psychological thinking of today. I know in my own life that after I began to meditate it suddenly became clear that the Bible and all the Holy Books are not telling children's stories; they are direct accounts of what happened to real people like us.

Kennett Rōshi: Yes, they are real accounts, very real. Here at Shasta we study the Buddhist Scriptures daily *in detail*, for I know that they are literally true. They are incredibly valuable and were obtained at death's door, not by special people unlike us, but by ordinary men and women who meditated deeply, dedicated themselves completely, and trained with enormous effort.

QUESTION: Had you ever read any works that have similar experiences to this prior to your having them?

Kennett Rōshi: No. I had owned *The Secret of the Golden Flower* for many years but not read it. The *Hui Ming Ching* and "Life of the Hasidim" I only discovered recently after I had almost finished the kenshō. Even then they were only discovered as a result of the researches of a number of people who were trying to find parallel works in other religions.

QUESTION: You included passages from Taoist and Judaic scriptures as well as referring to Buddhist sutras, and you have referred to the Christian mystics. Are you saying that this is a way to amalgamate the various religions into one?

Kennett Rōshi: No. It is good that there are many different religions; different people need different paths. It is just nice to know that we are already in the same place. People who think that they have left one religion for another have actually not moved from the hand of the Lord of the House.

QUESTION: Have these experiences changed your understanding or appreciation for Buddhist doctrine?

Kennett Rōshi: They *proved* Buddhist doctrine. Consider the eating of meat: you literally see the chain of dependent origination in action; you see the suffering of the animal; you feel it physically.

Monk: When I was on a trip recently, someone served chicken. As the platter was passed, I picked up the entire story of how the bird was slaughtered—its fright—everything. This was not my imagination; you can actually see and feel it. It was like having a corpse on the table.

Second Monk: When I worked logging during the summer I used to walk through the woods while the trees were being cut down, and it was exactly like being in a battlefield. Your whole outlook towards all of sentient existence really changes from this.

QUESTION: Is the process you described still going on?

Kennett Rōshi: Yes.

Monk: The process of training always goes on. A kenshō is not the end of training, it is a new beginning.

Lay Buddhist: When I was reading this, after I got over the grandeur of it, I saw that what Rōshi was doing was *just training*. She's just going on down the road.

Monk: The "gyate, gyate" of the Scripture of Great Wisdom is true: "going on, going on, always *becoming* Buddha."

267

GLOSSARY.

Abbreviations: ZEL, *Zen is Eternal Life;*
C, Chinese;
J, Japanese;
P, Pali;
S, Sanskrit.

ANANDA (J), Ānanda (S), the Buddha's personal attendant, who memorized the Buddha's discourses and passed them on as the Sutras. He was enlightened after the Buddha's death and became the second Patriarch, succeeding Makakashyo. See Denkōroku, chap. 3, in ZEL, p. 205.

ANCESTORS, those who have transmitted the truth of Buddhism. Also called Patriarchs. See Patriarchal line, ZEL, p. 284, and Denkōroku, pp. 199-264.

ANICCA (P), anitya (S), the universality of change. See Gyakudo-yōjinshu, ZEL, p. 123ff, and Uji, ZEL, p. 163ff.

ASURA (S), Titan, rebel god. Also one who tries to storm Heaven.

AVATAMSAKA SUTRA (S), Hua-yen Ching (C), Kegonkyo (J), one of the great Mahayana Sutras, containing a wide variety of material on all aspects of Buddhist training. Only a few short sections have been translated into English.

BODHIDHARMA, Indian monk who went to China and transmitted the Zen teaching. The 28th Patriarch in India and the first in China.

BODHISATTVA (S), one who undertakes the training to become a fully enlightened Buddha for the benefit of all beings, and does not train for his own liberation only. See ZEL, pp. 33-60.

BODHISATTVA VOW, the commitment to complete and endless training for the benefit of all beings, without reservations. There are many forms of Bodhisattva Vow emphasizing all the different aspects of training. See ZEL, pp. 33-60, 273-77, 346.

BUDDHA (S), literally, 'awakened;' one who is fully enlightened, having fulfilled the Bodhisattva training; especially Shakyamuni Buddha.

BUDDHA MIND, the mind without attachment and discrimination which is the real mind of all beings, although they themselves may not recognize it.

BUDDHA'S NOBLE TRUTHS, see Four Noble Truths.

CHIEF JUNIOR, one selected by the Abbot of a monastery to lead all trainees during the training period of one hundred days. At the end of this period he is tested in a special ceremony. See Kessei, ZEL, pp. 334-43; see also ZEL, Book I, chap. 9, pp. 68-8l.

COSMIC BUDDHA, the Buddha who appears in every place and time and in all beings; also called by various other names such as Vairocana Buddha, Amitabha Buddha, Dharmakaya, Buddha Nature, Lord of the House. It can be revealed by genuine training, but it cannot be explained as existing or not existing, or in any other dualistic way.

DAI KAIDŌ (J), Literally 'great hall of shadows;' the home of Buddha Nature within a being, where it remains hidden unless revealed by training. Although it is not spatial, it can manifest itself in the hara.

DEVA (S), demi-god or angel.

DHARMA (S), the teaching of the Buddha, the Truth.

DIAMOND SCRIPTURE, Vajracchedika Prajnaparamita
Sutra (S), one of the most important scriptures in
Zen, giving the teaching of emptiness in concise
form. The full title is 'The Scripture of Great Wisdom, the Diamond-Cutter.'

DŌGEN ZENJI, founder of Sōtō Zen in Japan, author
of *The Treasury Eye of the True Teaching*. In ZEL,
pp. 183-90.

EKŌ, offertory giving merit of ceremony or scripture
recitation to someone else. See ZEL, Book IV,
especially pp. 306-11.

ENLIGHTENMENT, Nirvana (S), Bodhi (S), religious
realization or understanding.

ENLIGHTENMENT BY OTHERS, Sravaka-bodhi (S),
becoming enlightened as a result of hearing the
teaching and putting it into practice to realise no-
self but not the emptiness of all things, without
undertaking the Bodhisattva practice. The first
level in Hinayana, the other being single enlightenment. Both of these levels retain the idea of
training for oneself, which is abandoned in the
Mahayana practice of the Bodhisattva path.

FIVE LAWS OF THE UNIVERSE, the operation of
the universe divided into five laws. The laws, in
one form, are: (1) the laws of the physical world—
that the world is not answerable to one's will;
(2) the laws of the organic world—that all things
flow; (3) the laws of morality—that karma is inexorable; (4) the laws of the Dharma—that evil is
vanquished and good prevails; (5) the laws of
mind—that of the will to enlightenment.

FOUR NOBLE TRUTHS, the summary of the Dharma
taught by Shakyamuni Buddha soon after his enlightenment: (1) All existence is filled with suffering; (2) Suffering is caused by clinging to things
material, spiritual or sensual; (3) Suffering can be

transcended and Nirvana realized here and now, and (4) The way to end suffering is by the daily practice of serious religious training and the keeping of the Buddhist Precepts.

FŪGEN (J), Samantabhadra (S), the Bodhisattva 'Full of Virtue' who symbolizes the second, on-going kenshô. See 'Activity in the Heart of Fûgen,' ZEL, pp. 43-50. Fûgen's training and vows are given in the Avatamsaka Sutra.

FULL-LOTUS POSITION, the meditation position used by the Buddha, with each foot placed on the opposite thigh. See *Zen Meditation*, The Journal of Shasta Abbey, Nov.-Dec. 1976.

GASSHŌ (J), holding the hands up with palms together.

GOI (J), the Five Ranks of the relationship between appearance and reality, from worldly mind to enlightenment, as taught by Tôzan Ryokai and his successors. The next to last stage in Rinzai Zen Kôan training, the last being the Buddhist Precepts.

HAISEKI (J), mat in front of an altar where the celebrant in a service stands and bows.

HALF-LOTUS POSITION, meditation position with one foot on the opposite thigh. See *Zen Meditation*, The Journal of Shasta Abbey, Nov.-Dec., 1976.

HANAMATSURI (J), 'flower festival,' The Buddha's birthday, May 8, celebrated on December 25 at Shasta Abbey. See ZEL, pp. 307-8.

HARA (J), triangle formed from the base of the sternum, down the sides of the rib cage extending downwards to the navel.

HŌKYOZAMMAI (J), Pao-ching San-wei (C), The Most Excellent Mirror-Samàdhi, by Tôzan Ryokai, a scripture recited daily in Zen monasteries. ZEL, pp. 280-83.

HOLY LOTUS SCRIPTURE, Saddharma Pundarika (S), the first of the great Mahayana Sutras, revealing the way of Bodhisattva training for all beings.

HONDŌ (J), hall where services are conducted.

HOSSU (J), symbol of the priest's compassion.

HUNGRY GHOSTS, preta (S), spirits with bloated bellies and throats so small that they cannot swallow food; people whose attachments make it impossible for them to receive the teaching of the Buddhas. See Segaki (Feeding the Hungry Ghosts), ZEL, pp. 358-59.

IMPREGNATIONS, vasana (S), remnants of karma from the past which must still be dealt with after the roots of greed, hate and delusion have been cut. Even though no new karma is created, the effects of past karma remain.

IRON MAN, Vajrasattva (S), the appearance of the Buddha Nature which shows that it is indestructible and is not affected by birth and death or indeed anything that may happen. See Denkōroku, chap. 1, ZEL, pp. 199-202.

JŌDŌ (J), testing of an abbot by question and answer as he stands on the altar as the living Buddha. Held in conjunction with the testing of his Chief Junior. See ZEL, pp. 399-40.

KAIDŌ (J), see Dai Kaidō.

KAISHAKU (J), wooden clappers used as signals during Zen ceremonies.

KANZEON BOSATSU (J), Avalokitesvara Bodhisattva (S), Kuan-shi-yin, Kuan Yin (C), also Kannon (J), "Hearing the calls of the world." Kanzeon is the Bodhisattva who personifies Great Compassion and Mercy which arises as a result of true Training. She is depicted on the right hand of Amitabha Buddha often holding a lotus blossom. There are also Kanzeon statues with many arms expressing

the different ways in which trainees must help
other beings and with many heads, symbolizing
total awareness; the Heart of Kanzeon is the third
stage in Zen training and is the beginning of real
spirituality.

KARMA (S), kamma (P), action or cause and effect.
The law of MORAL cause and effect; the third of
the Five Laws of the Universe. All actions of body,
speech and mind produce karma which continues
in the future and which may be seen as good (ku-
sala karma) or bad (akusala karma). The Law of
Karma is inexorable but there is no external law-
giver; each person is totally responsible for all of
his actions and their consequences.

KENSHŌ (J), "To see into one's own nature." The
experience of enlightenment, satori. Bodhidharma
called it "a special transmission outside the scriptures, not based on words or letters; pointing
directly to the heart of man, enabling him to see
into his own true nature and realize Buddhahood."
Through diligent meditation and training, a trainee
can directly realize his own Buddha Mind. This is
completely beyond all intellectual, philosophical
or metaphysical thinking. In Rinzai, the kenshō or
satori experience is the principal aim, being em-
phasized above all else; however in Sōtō, the crucial
thing is to completely unify training and enlightenment in daily life; it is not merely a matter of
enlightenment experiences, but rather of making
one's whole life the Buddha's life.

KESA (J), kasaya (S), the Buddhist priest's robe. When
Shakyamuni Buddha left his palace, he crossed the
river and threw off his royal garments. He then
took some rags, sewed them together to form a
simple square robe worn over the left shoulder,
and called it a kesa. The kesa symbolizes departing

from the world in order to realize Nirvana. Priests in all the Buddhist traditions wear some form of kesa. The robe is always made up of small rectangular pieces of material sewn together and may have five, seven, nine or more stripes depending on the tradition. In Sōtō Zen temples, a seven-striped kesa is worn during meditation, formal meals, and services. During work, a rakhsu—a smaller version of five stripes worn around the neck— is worn. Junior trainees normally wear black robes and at Transmission trainees are given a colored kesa, usually brown or orange. Abbots often wear purple or on special occasions, gold brocade. The colors, however, vary greatly from temple to temple. The wagesa is another form of kesa. See also Rakhsu.

KŌAN (J), k'ung-an (C), 'case.' 1. The circumstantial catalyst from which the delusion and enlightenment of a being results. A kōan when completely understood contains both cause and effect. 2. The problem of Training and Enlightenment as it arises naturally in daily life, where intellect is incapable of handling it properly. 3. The popular historical opinion of a kōan is the account of the circumstances of someone becoming enlightened, and the problem they were faced with at the time. 4. At the present time the term kōan is popularly used to denote that which demonstrates enlightenment in order to teach Zen. The meaning of the term as used in this book, however, is the deep and complete one first mentioned, embracing both cause and effect.

KYOJŪKAIMON (J), Keizan Zenji's explanation of the Buddhist Precepts, read whenever the Precepts are given. In ZEL, pp. 265-68.

LAW, Dharma.

LORD OF THE HOUSE, Buddha in each being, Buddha Nature, Cosmic Buddha, Who is not explicable in terms of existence and non-existence or self and other.

LOTUS SCRIPTURE, see Holy Lotus Scripture.

MAKAKASHYO (J), Mahakasyapa (S), the Buddha's chief disciple, leader of the Sangha after the Buddha's death. See Denkôroku, ZEL, pp. 202-l0.

MAKYO (J), any unusual phenomena or mental or physical attachments which cause a person to stumble in his single-mindedness in *continuing* his training. Training has to be continuous both before, during and after kenshô. Anything that halts the rhythm of this continuous movement is makyo.

MANDALA (S), mandara (J), a diagram, usually circular, expressing a religious view of the universe through symbols or portraits of Buddhas and Bodhisattvas. Mandalas are used mostly in Shingon and Tibetan Buddhism.

MARA (S), the tempter, the personification of makyo.

NENJU (J), Meditation Hall Closing Ceremony. ZEL, pp. 304-5.

NOBLE EIGHTFOLD PATH, Arya-asta-anga-marga (S), the path of Buddhist Training which leads to the end of suffering. Explained at Plate XXXIX.

NYOI (J), a wooden or jade staff occasionally with a twisted dragon around its length, carried by a celebrant during ceremonies, symbolizing the nyoi jewel. The staff can also be in the shape of a lotus blossom representing the compassion of Kanzeon.

OBON (J), the time of Segaki in Japan, usually July 15, called the Festival of Lanterns.

OX-HERDING PICTURES, a sequence of ten pictures with accompanying verses, symbolizing the stages of Buddhist training. They can be found in *Zen*

Flesh, Zen Bones, by Rev. Nyogen Senzaki and Paul Reps.

PATRIARCH, see Ancestors.

PRECEPTS, kai (J), sila (S), the ways of living that are in accordance with the Dharma. The second Paramita. One of the fundamental practices of the Bodhisattva training along with meditation, compassion and wisdom. They are given at Plate VIII.

QUIETISM, a spiritual disease which arises as a result of an improper attitude of mind. In Zen it is characterized by attachment to sitting meditation, inefficiency in work, and irresponsibility. It is also characterized by lack of will and spirit, and a desire to retreat from life.

RAKHSU (J), a small version of the Buddhist priest's robe. See illustration on Plate XXVII.

RŌSHI (J), "reverend master." A title of a Zen Master. This title is conferred by a Master only upon his worthiest disciples. However it can also be used simply as an honorary title of respect. The word "sensei" (teacher) is also used.

SANSARA (S), the world of suffering, birth and death.

SANDŌKAI (J), a Zen scripture by Sekitō Kisen. In ZEL, pp. 279-80.

SANGE (J), "contrition," "confession," "repentence." The sincere recognition of all that is wrong within one and the acceptance of one's past karma. Sange is the true source of religious humility and a principal gateway to enlightenment. Zazen opens the door to Sange, since by sitting still within one's own heart, one ceases to turn away from seeing one's own true nature with the straightforward mind. The Sange verse, found in Dōgen's "Shushōgi" and the ordination ceremonies, comes from the Fūgen chapter of the *Avatamsaka Scripture* and says, "All the evil committed by me is caused by beginningless greed, hate and delusion. All the evil is committed by my body, speech and mind. I now confess everything wholeheartedly." The formal Sange ceremony is done during each Jūkai Sesshin.

SANGHA (S), the community of those who follow the Buddha's teaching. Sangha refers sometimes to both priests and laymen, and sometimes to priests only.

SCRIPTURE OF GREAT WISDOM, Hannya-Shingyo (J), Prajna-paramita-hrdaya-sutra (S), also known as the *Heart Scripture* as it is considered to be the essence or heart of the Great Wisdom Scriptures. Recited daily in all Zen temples, it teaches the immaculacy or emptiness of all things.

SEGAKI (J), feeding the hungry spirits, a ceremony performed annually for all those who have died the previous year without having become enlightened, or on special occasions as needed. Held at Shasta Abbey on October 31. In ZEL, pp. 358-39.

SHAKYAMUNI BUDDHA, founder of Buddhism in the 6th century B.C. See ZEL, pp. 3-7, 199-204.

SHŌNAWASHYU (J), Sanavasa (S), the third Patriarch in India, successor to Ananda. See ZEL, pp. 2ll-18.

SHŌSAN (J), ceremony similar to Jōdō held every two weeks in Zen monasteries, in which all trainees bring their kōans to the Abbot.

SINGLE ENLIGHTENMENT, pratyeka-bodhi (S), enlightenment reached by oneself alone and not passed on to others. The second level of Hinayana.

SKHANDAS (S), "aggregates." In Buddhism, all of existence is categorized into five aggregates or heaps. They are (1) form or matter; (2) sensation or feelings; (3) thought or perceptions; (4) impulses and activity, (5) consciousness. When the skhandas are viewed through ignorance a false notion of a self is created. Seen through the eyes of meditation, the five skhandas are "void, unstained and clean."

SURANGAMA (S), Ryogonkyo (J), a Mahayana Sutra, much used in Zen. Excerpted in ZEL, pp. 52-54.

SUTRA (S), any Buddhist scripture spoken by a Buddha or Bodhisattva; usually attributed to Shakyamuni Buddha.

TAOISM, the teachings of Lao-tzu, Chuang-tzu and their successors.

TATHAGATA (S), Buddha.

TEN BUDDHAS. The names of the Ten Buddhas are recited in many Zen ceremonies. Note that the "Ten Buddhas" include scriptures, Bodhisattvas and Patriarchs, indicating every form of Buddha.

THREE TREASURES, Buddha, Dharma and Sangha.

TITAN ASURAS, see Asuras.

TRANSMISSION, Dembō (J). In the Zen tradition, the Truth is passed down heart to heart and this has been called the Transmission of Mind or Dharma. This Transmission is beyond all words and concepts and only takes place when the Master and disciple are One in the Buddha Mind. The first example of the Transmission is the story in the *Denkōroku* of Makakashyo, the First Patriarch.

UNSUI (J), "cloud (un) water (sui)," a priest trainee, Buddhist monk. A person, male or female, who has dedicated his or her life to Buddhist training and has undergone the ordination ceremony (to-kudō). The word "unsui" expresses that the trainee must be as the clouds which wander freely obstructed by nothing, and like water which flows. An unsui is someone who is trying to do something about himself.

VASANA (S), see Impregnations.

ZAZEN (J), 'sitting meditation,' meditation in which one sits still, not trying to think and not trying *not* to think. See "Zazen Rules" in this book.

ZENJI (J), ch'an-shih (C), "Zen Master." In the T'ang dynasty in China the title Zenji applied first to any practitioner of meditation and later only to eminent teachers. However, in present-day Japan the title is bestowed by the emperor on only a few of the Chief Abbots of the largest Zen monasteries.

ABOUT THE AUTHOR.

Rōshi Jiyu Kennett is a Zen Master trained in the Sōtō Zen tradition and is the Abbess and Spiritual Director of Shasta Abbey, a Zen seminary and training monastery at Mt. Shasta, California. Born in 1924, in England, Rōshi Kennett became a Buddhist in the Theravādin tradition. She was later introduced to Rinzai Zen by D. T. Suzuki in London where she held membership in, and lectured at, the London Buddhist Society. She received her formal education at Trinity College of Music, London, and Durham University.

In January, 1962, Rōshi Kennett was ordained in the Chinese Rinzai tradition in Malacca, Malaysia, and then continued on to Japan to study Sōtō (Ts'ao Tung) Zen at Dai Hon Zan Sōji-ji Temple, one of the two head temples of the Sōtō Zen school of Japan where she became the personal disciple of the Chief Abbot, the Very Reverend Chisan Kōhō Zenji. After several years of training she became head of the Foreign Guest Department being in charge of instructing the many Westerners who came to the temple. Rōshi Kennett was Transmitted by Kōhō Zenji and was installed as Abbess of Unpuku-ji Temple, in Mie Prefecture, Japan, where she taught her own Western disciples. She also earned the Sei Degree (a priesthood degree that requires at least five years of continuous study, roughly equivalent to a Christian Doctor of Divinity) whilst at Dai Hon Zan Sōji-ji and was granted a Sanzen License.

In November, 1969, accompanied by two Western disciples, Rōshi Kennett came to San Francisco on a lecture tour. The Zen Mission Society was founded the following year and moved to Mt. Shasta for the founding of Shasta Abbey.

In addition to being Abbess of Shasta Abbey, Rōshi Kennett has been an instructor at the University of California Extension, in Berkeley, since 1972, is on the faculty of the California Institute of Transpersonal Psychology and has lectured at universities throughout the world. She has founded numerous Zen temples and meditation groups throughout the United States, Canada and England. She has also authored *Zen is Eternal Life* (Dharma Publishing, 1976), formerly published as *Selling Water by the River* (Pantheon, 1972), a manual of Zen Buddhist training.

SHASTA ABBEY,
HEADQUARTERS OF THE
REFORMED SŌTŌ ZEN CHURCH.

Shasta Abbey, headquarters of the Reformed Sōtō Zen Church, is a seminary and training monastery for the Zen Buddhist priesthood. Located on fifteen acres of forest land north of the city of Mt. Shasta, California, the Abbey was established in November, 1970, by Rōshi Jiyu Kennett who is the Abbess and Spiritual Director. The Abbey provides training for both members of the priesthood and lay students; there is no discrimination with regard to sex; both men and women may enter the priesthood and become full priests and teachers. At the time of going to print, April, 1977, there are thirty priest-trainees in residence. The priest training program is approved by the California Department of Education, approved for Veterans Administration and Social Security benefits and for attendance by foreign students.

The Abbey's lay training program is open to serious lay students who wish to undergo Zen Buddhist training for any period of time; there are week-long sesshins, introductory and advanced weekend retreats throughout the year. In addition to the above there are the following religious services:— reception into the Buddhist Church (lay ordination), naming ceremonies for children, weddings, funerals and memorial services; the Abbey has a cemetery available to members and other Buddhists. Private spiritual direction (sanzen) is available at all times; all letters concerning serious religious questions are answered.

Shasta Abbey publishes a monthly magazine, the *Journal of Shasta Abbey*, which includes articles by Rōshi Kennett, priests of the Abbey and others on various aspects of Zen training. The Abbey also publishes special booklets from time to time; these include "Zen Meditation" and "Becoming a Buddhist."

Branch communities and affiliated meditation groups are located in Berkeley and Chico, California; Cottage Grove, Portland and Ashland, Oregon; London, Hexham and Penaluna, England. Retreats led by priests of Shasta Abbey are occasionally held in Vancouver and Toronto, Canada, and in the Los Angeles, California, area.

For more information please contact Shasta Abbey, Mt. Shasta, California, 96067; telephone 916/ 926-4208.